Letter To My Mother

Reflections on the
Christian Reformed Church in North America

by
Edward Heerema

Author of
RB A Prophet in the Land

ISBN 0-9626955-0-5
Library of Congress Catalog Card Number 90-093205

Copyright © 1990 by
Edward Heerema

Published by
Rev. Edward Heerema, Th.M.
619 S.E. 32nd St.
Cape Coral, Florida 33904

Printed in United States of America

 PINE HILL PRESS, INC.
Freeman, S. Dak. 57029

Jesus, with Thy Church abide;
Be her Savior, Lord and Guide,
While on earth her faith is tried:
We Beseech Thee, hear us.

May her lamp of truth be bright;
Bid her bear aloft its light
Through the realms of pagan night:
We beseech Thee, hear us.

Thomas B. Pollock

Contents

Preface vii

1 Dear Mother – 1

2 1924 – Unfinished Business 5

3 1952 – Watershed 23

4 44 – A Stumbling Church 35

5 44-1973 – The Church Stumbles Again 43

6 Does the Christian Reformed Church Have A
  Church Order? 53

7 Creation Or Evolution 73

8 More Marks Of A Church In Trouble 95

9 From Confusion and Uncertainty To What? 111

Postscript 124

Appendix A – The Florida Overture 127

Appendix B – The Church's Witness And The Issue Of
Women In Office 131

Preface

For some time I have felt that some one should write a book or extended pamphlet on the current state of affairs in my church, the Christian Reformed Church in North America. That state of affairs presents a picture in which confident and steadfast assurance seems to have given way to confusion and uncertainty. Many members are no longer sure of their church, no longer sure of what she stands for in a mixed-up world. What do her doctrinal standards mean in today's world? And the church is polarized; it is not a united body. Can we determine how the state of affairs came about.

Some forty years ago church historian John Kromminga published his book entitled *The Christian Reformed Church—A Study In Orthodoxy*. At that time Kromminga could say that the Christian Reformed Church was "substantially" the same as it was during its entire history. He could also say that, "far from losing its vitality, the denomination has vastly increased the influence which it wields" (p. 14). He concluded his study with these comments: "There are those who say that the Christian Reformed Church is merely a few decades behind the other denominations in the loss of its orthodoxy. The perusal of competent histories of the other denominations lends some credence to this theory. The fact remains that the Christian Reformed Church is today an outstanding example of continued orthodoxy. What the future holds in store for it time alone can tell." (p. 225).

That was 1949. Those "few decades" have now passed. We stand in that future of which Kromminga spoke. What is the state of orthodoxy in the Christian Reformed Church today? What follows is an effort to answer that question. This result of my effort is sent out in the awareness that one piece of writing by one observer can hardly do justice to such a complex and delicate subject. So with it goes the hope that further reflection by others will follow to help the church rediscover itself.

The book comes in the form of a letter. This format has good precedent, of course, in the writings of the great apostle to the churches. This format makes for warmth and intimacy, qualities quite in order in a letter addressed to my spiritual mother and referring to my brothers and sisters in the church. Also, a letter bears a personal stamp. That stamp is evident in the following chapters in the use of personal pronouns in the first person singular. This book is not a joint effort. The opinions and judgments within the frame of the ensuing letter are those of the author; he does not speak for some group.

This personal quality shows itself also in the choice of material. The author has made his own selection of subjects to be discussed in this study. However, this selection should not be viewed as being merely arbitrary. Those matters were chosen which were seen as contributing to and as illustrating decay in theological reflection in the church. Of course, the likelihood is that no two authors would make exactly the same selection.

This personal factor in the choice of subject matter is especially apparent in the considerable space devoted in Chapter 6 ("Does The Christian Reformed Church Have A Church Order?") to an overture that originated with the consistory of my church, the Cape Coral Christian Reformed Church. This overture dealt with a very important aspect of the question of the place of the Bible in today's church. I was very familiar with this piece of church business and its history in the church courts. I regret that the chapter is long, and perhaps makes for tedious reading. I felt I had to be detailed in the account of this overture's life and death in the church in order to show that it is highly appropriate to wonder whether the Christian Reformed Church does in actual practice have a Church Order.

It is my sincere hope that many who are not members of the Christian Reformed Church will read what I have to say. This part of the body of Christ has long enjoyed a reputation for solid Biblical preaching and principled loyalty to Jesus Christ and his Kingdom. It should be a matter of real concern to members of other Christian groups when a church with such a history is perceived as drifting from its Biblical and confessional anchorage. Furthermore, the concerns, needs and heartaches of one part of the body of Christ are much like the concerns, needs and heartaches of every other part. Are we not all one body?

One item of contemporary history must be observed as this book is read. There are in the ensuing pages a number of references to *The Banner* and its editorial policies and utterances. The reader should note that this official church magazine underwent a change of editors in the autumn of 1989. None of the references in the book is to the work of the editor who took office then.

A word of hearty thanks is due those who read all or parts of the manuscript of this Letter. Many helpful suggestions were made, and I have tried to do justice to them. I also want to thank those who responded to letters from me in which I asked for information about events, attitudes and developments in the church.

I earnestly hope that those who are disposed to disagree with what I have to say will at least read this book with some care. Disunity has become marked and sharp in the Christian Reformed Church. There is an unwillingness to listen to others who may disagree with a position taken, and polarization deepens. If there is to be healing it must begin with serious listening and sustained reflection – and much praying for each other.

Edward Heerema
Cape Coral, Florida

CHAPTER 1
Dear Mother—

For some time I have been wanting to write to you. Certain things have been troubling me and I feel I would not be true to you or to myself if I did not speak to you about them.

As I write I must make something very clear. This is that I hope you will understand beyond a shadow of doubt that I love you, Mother. How could I do otherwise? You have been all that a mother could be to me, and more. I can say best what I feel toward you by stating simply that, like a true mother, you were always there for me. You were there when I was born, you were there when I was baptized, you were there as I grew up, you were there when I had the beautiful experience of professing before men my faith in Jesus Christ as my Savior and Lord. You have been there through the times when my faith wavered. Even when I departed from the family for a time to make my home with another family, you were always still there. And when I returned into the family circle I found you still there, still always dependable, always a source of strength and stability in the ebb and flow of life. I could always count on you. You were strong and trustworthy.

I so earnestly wish that things were still that way. Nothing would give me greater joy than to be able to say in all sincerity that you are still the strong, wholly dependable and altogether loving mother that you always were to me. But Mother, it deeply grieves me to have to say that I don't find you today as I have previously found you. I can't be sure about you. And many others in the family feel the same way.

Yes, many in the family are concerned about you, and many are sorely troubled. There are even those who feel you are no longer what you once were and so they consider leaving the family. Others leave the family rather readily to join other groups because it appears to them that our family no longer has its recognizable character. They seem to think that many families are about the same as ours, so why stay with ours. Our family

1

used to have an ethnic distinctiveness, but that is no longer the case. But has our family retained a more basic distinctiveness? Apparently quite a number think not.

Some in the family have spoke freely of winds of change blowing through and around the family. Others say ours is a family in transition. What changes? Changes to what? Transition to what? That is not at all clear. Is our family to be likened to a ship that has lots it rudder and is at the mercy of the tossing seas of history?

I read an interesting, throughly documented book about you recently. It is entitled *Dutch Calvinism In Modern America* (1984). The book left me puzzled and uncertain. It speaks of two streams of influence in the recent history of the family, namely, the Confessionalists (Antitheticals, Conservatives) and the Progressives. This question stuck with me: just where does the family stand? Is the last word on the family to be this – a house divided?

This question becomes very insistent when I look at the weekly letter you send out to the members of the family. In the past several years the tone and content of this weekly communication changed. These weekly letters no longer gave the family clear guidance. Whatever may have been one's opinion of the weekly letters in the past, one thing was generally quite clear, namely, that the letters, being an official voice in the family, set forth, defended and applied those positions which the family had always agreed on as basic to its life. That was no longer the case, and the family is suffering. Division, disagreement and uncertainty were being promoted by an instrument which has always been regarded as a banner of a unified family. This is a particularly sad feature of our family's life, Mother. The cries of distress among the family members at the letter's performance appeared in almost every issue.

Mother, I am not writing to you as one who is resistant to all change. Not at all. Stagnant traditionalists are of no real help in a church family that wants to grow. Such people, it is sometimes said, have not had a fresh thought in ten years. At the same time we must beware of those who use the very worthy phrase "a Reformed church must always be reforming" to mean that a Reformed church must always be changing. A family like ours can change so much that it is no longer indentifiable, either by its own members or by others. Not a few in the family have said that they have been in Sunday gatherings that they could not recognize as part of the family. Others have been at Lord's Day gatherings where the leader seemed to think he had to entertain the assembled folk. Still others have lamented that liturgical manipulation, innovations and gimmicks have taken the place of sound preaching and reflective worshiper response. It seems, Mother, that it is not uncommon to find a subtle shift in emphasis from concentration on the greatness of God and the grandeur of his grace in Christ to preoccupation with the shifting needs and feelings of people. No, Mother, I do not plead for a coldly doctrinaire neglect of these needs and feelings, but rather for a vision of them in the light of primary emphasis on God, his Word and the warmth of his matchless grace.

Mother, it seems sadly clear that the family is no longer united. We are divided, divided and unclear as to just who we are and where we are going. Some in the family do pretty much as they please in matters of proper order. At times the very important official instrument by which we are bound together in confession (called the Form of Subscription) has been ignored and even ridiculed. Then again items in our statements of faith have been questioned and attacked in disregard of the proper procedure that has been set up for dealing with sincere efforts to amend or correct our statements of faith. In a situation like this there is always the possibility that certain people in positions of leadership will feel that they have to take charge for the good of the family as they see it. In the words of a familiar commercial they say, "Leave the driving to us." Then bureaucracy asserts itself and our very character as a family of responsible believers is compromised. Of late the family has even been considering a serious proposal that the direction of its affairs be placed in the hands of a powerful central committee.

I think I have said enough, Mother, to make clear my keen concern for the well-being of our family. It is with no pleasure that I write thus. Surely I take no pleasure in causing you distress. But write I must. I cannot do otherwise. A beautiful family fellowship is threatened with disruption and dismemberment. Many hearts are heavy, Mother. Sincere members of the family who love you feel they, for reasons of conscience, may have to leave our community of believers, and this saddens all of us. Some of the troubled ones may have themselves to blame for not accepting necessary change, change that is in keeping with the teaching of God's Word. But many of those who are deeply concerned about the family's welfare are alert and well-read followers of our Lord. They cannot be and may not be arrogantly dismissed as ill-informed troublemakers or stagnant traditionalists. They love the Word; they love the teachings of the church. The family cannot ignore or offend these members without great harm to itself. All would do well to heed the clarion call of a great prophet of the past who declared, "To the law and to the testimony! If they do not speak according to this word, they have no light of dawn" (Isaiah 8:20).

Thank you for listening to me, Mother. I shall be writing in more detail about some of the matters referred to above, and other matters as well. Please remember, Mother, I write because I love you. And may God yet give you good health.

I want to be and remain

Your faithful son,
Edward

CHAPTER 2
1924—Unfinished Business

The cozily attractive Asolo Theater was the setting. The play being presented was one of America's most popular ones, *Life With Father*, by Clarence Day. The wit in the play was sharp. Again and again the audience burst into hearty laughter. But there was something else about the play. It was laced with profanity, heavy profanity. God's name was repeatedly used in a manner that was totally devoid of the honor and respect due that holy name.

Without question the production received high marks under the criteria by which such things are judged. It was, by most standards, a superior piece of literature in its genre. Surely it was highly entertaining to the audience that night in Sarasota.

Now a question has to be raised about that highly popular play. Was this play with its repeated misuse of God's name an illustration of God's common grace? The question can be put succinctly: are we to see God's grace in a production that blatantly blasphemes God?

For another illustration of this same problem we turn to the writings of the greatest exponent of the doctrine of common grace, namely, Abraham Kuyper, whose three volume work, *De Gemeene Gratie*, is the outstanding text on the subject. Kuyper takes the teaching of total depravity very seriously. Sin, upon entering the human experience, in Paradise, so influenced the mind of man that it was darkened, its knowledge bound to develop increasingly as a matter of sham and self-deception. Yet, actually such is not the case. Knowledge among men has considerable validity. This is due to common grace. We must do justice to both realities, that of the darkening power of sin in man's life, and that of the influence of common grace. Under these terms Kuyper drops some names of intellectual giants who have made great contributions to knowledge.

5

He names four "stars of the highest magnitude"—Plato, Aristotle, Kant and Darwin.[1]

The name of Darwin catches our eye. Due to common grace operating on the minds of men the scholar most commonly associated with the theory of evolution is here acclaimed. Yet elsewhere Kuyper has described Darwin's theory as "purely atheistic," as "the legitimate daughter" of "the pantheistic tendency of our age." Kuyper is further quoted as saying that "this whole pantheistic stream has left a poisonous slime upon the shore, and it is in Darwin's evolution theory that this slime reveals its power."[2]

Naturally the question arises: how can a theory that is atheistic, that denies that God of all grace, be itself a product of the common grace the God bestows on mankind? The question can again be stated succinctly: are we to see God's grace in a conception that denies the very being of God? It is questions like these that press themselves upon us we reflect on a subject of which C. Van Til has said "that, theoretically, the question is exceedingly complicated."[3]

What Happened In 1924?

So far as our present interest is concerned three things happened at the synod of the Christian Reformed Church in the year 1924.

In the first place three points on the matter of common grace were adopted, three points that were set up in answer to those in the church who would deny the reality of common grace. The synod declared (1) that there is, besides the saving grace of God, also a certain favor or grace of God which he shows to his creatures in general; (2) that there is the restraint of sin in the life of the individual and in society; and (3) that the unregenerate are capable of doing so-called civic

---

[1]*Common Grace and Science and Art*, the last section of Volume III of Kuyper's work *De Gemeene Gratie*. The section has its own separate pagination. The present reference is to page 12 of this section.

[2]"Abraham Kuyper: Cultural Critic" by Edward E. Ericson, Jr. in *Calvin Theological Journal*, Nov. 1987, p. 218.

[3]"Common Grace" by C. Van Til in *Westminster Theological Journal*, Nov. 1946, p. 84.

righteousness. The synod furnished what it saw as scriptural and confessional warrant for each of these points.

In the second place the synod said plainly that it did not regard its three-point declaration as an adequate statement of the doctrine of common grace. Further study and development of the doctrine was urged upon ministers and professors. Indeed, the synod asked that many participate in such study.

In the third place the synod issued a solemn warning with respect to the teaching of common grace. It warned against the ever-present threat of growing worldliness on the part of the church members and that the tenet of common grace should not be allowed to increase that threat. "It is imperative," the synod said, "for the church, to guard the principle involved and, while upholding the doctrine of common grace, to maintain tooth and nail the spiritual-ethical antithesis."

What ever came of this urgent appeal for further study? Not much, regrettably. There was a flurry of activity in the late forties and fifties but not much came of it. There was one effort that looked promising, but it petered out. In 1953 the magazine *Torch and Trumpet* (later named *The Outlook*) launched what was proposed as a significant effort to develop the subject of common grace. Four men were appointed to form a Common Grace Commission. Their plan was to publish articles on the subject by various authors, to study relevant scriptural passages and then to formulate the doctrine "in some detail." The project got off the ground with considerable enthusiasm, but then it was aborted. Just why it was dropped is not clear. Perhaps it was for the best. The four men on the Commission were all busy pastors, and it is doubtful that they would have had the time to do the research and careful formulation that this complex subject called for.

So as a matter of fact very little has been done in the Christian Reformed Church in response to the urgent request for further study and explication voiced in 1924. This is indeed deeply regrettable. Common grace is a fascinating subject. It is a multi-faceted subject which interlocks with many other significant elements of the Christian faith. And in speaking of common grace we are dealing with a glorious matter, namely, that of *grace,* a theme which in its richest meaning always warms the heart of the Christian and gives wings to his spirit. Furthermore, as Abraham Kuyper pointed out again and again, in common grace we have a teaching by means of which we avoid two extremes that can easily be tempting pitfalls for the Christian, namely, that of escape from the world or world-flight, and that of losing oneself in the world or world-conformity.

Of course, the comment may be made that much of the membership in the church is not interested in doctrinal study. Sad to say, that comment is most likely correct. Many members of the church have very little patience with an examination of the fine points of any doctrinal issue. However, though theological discussion can at times seem to be arcane, interminable and boring, the church may never bow to the notion that questions of doctrine are unimportant and irrelevant. To bow to such notions would be to strike a blow at the very core of Christianity, which is the conviction that truth is always basic to life. That is so because our life and faith flow forth from a Word, the Word of God, the Word of truth.

Furthermore, in common grace we have a teaching that has been embraced by most Reformed theologians from John Calvin on. In his work *Calvin On Common Grace* Herman Kuiper cites passages from a number of lesser known Reformed authors in their teaching of common grace. In addition the following well-known exponents of the teaching can be named; Jonathan Edwards, Charles Hodge, A. A. Hodge, H. Bavinck, A. Kuyper, V. Hepp, L. Berkhof, John Murray and R. B. Kuiper. So we are dealing with a matter that has been important to many leaders in the Reformed family of churches.

At the same time we must note that many questions relating to the teaching of common grace have not been answered. There is unfinished business here. Herman Kuiper lists a number of questions that have not been resolved. He concludes his book with an Appendix whose final words are these: "To be sure, all the leading spokesmen of Reformed Theology are agreed that there is a non-saving grace which is common to the elect and other sin-cursed creatures. But there is a marked difference of opinion among them with respect to various important questions touching this common grace."[4]

---

[4]Herman Kuiper, *Calvin on Common Grace*, Grand Rapids, Smitter Book Company, 1928. Appendix, p. xv.

Kuiper's book was published in 1928, four years after the pronouncement of the sketchy three points referred to earlier. Twenty five years later church historian John H. Kromminga, in referring to "certain differences" in the Christian Reformed Church, wrote as follows: "In our opinion the general nature of the differences can be ascertained, although they are not easy to define in brief terms. They may be viewed from various angles, *one of the most important of which is that of common grace.*"[5] This laconic statement begged for specifics and amplification, but that very lack in some measure underscored the fact of the unfinished business of 1924.

A much later commentary on the state of the church speaks more pointedly. In 1986 a professor of Religion and Theology at Calvin College wrote as follows: "Today the CRC has a strong institution and organization at the top. Because that top has been taken possession of by what I shall today call the Mind of Common Grace (Dr. Henry Stob gave it the self-congratulatory designation of 'the Positive Mind'), the CRC is being severed from its moorings and increasingly accommodated to the dominant mind of the mainline Protestant denominations in the US and the World Council of Churches. This fact is evident in many areas of the church's life, and so it is also evident in the church's use and abuse of the Bible . . . The Mind of Common Grace has become the dominant mind of the CRC's leadership. Though the Mind of the Antithesis won a battle over higher criticism in 1922, it lost the war in 1924, at least in the higher educational institutions of the CRC."[6]

The lack of more precise definition of the teaching of common grace is the more distressing because there is danger associated with this teaching. Abraham Kuyper was aware of

---

[5]*Yearbook of the Christian Reformed Church 1953*, p. 201. Italics added.

[6]Henry Vander Goot, "The Bible in the C.R.C. Today," *The Outlook*. Jan. 1986, pp. 8-10. Do we wish to set the Mind of Common Grace over against the mind of the Antithesis, as Dr. Vander Goot does here? Both "minds" are essential elements in the "mind" of a Reformed church. This is the view that came to expression in the warning against the misuse of the teaching of common grace by the Synod of 1924, a warning cited earlier in this chapter. Cf. also Heerema, *RB A Prophet In The Land*, pp. 210-211.

this danger, as he made clear in the Foreword to his three-volume work. In Kuyper's day there were critics who had serious misgivings about his teachings. One critic stated that Kuyper's formulation promoted "a process of acute secularization within Christianity."[7] A recent publication has raised a similar alert. "A word of caution also needs to be raised in the Reformed community," writes John Bolt, "because some of the proponents of common grace on occasion tend simply to 'baptize' all secular culture. The doctrine of common grace must not be used to obscure and obliterate the antithesis between the people of God and the 'world' also in their respective cultural activity."[8]

Earlier in its history the Christian Reformed Church demonstrated its awareness of the dangers associated with the doctrine of common grace in the celebrated Janssen case. Dr. Ralph Janssen was in many ways a brilliant scholar, one of the best educated men in the church in the first quarter of the century. He was professor of Old Testament in the Theological School (now Calvin Theological Seminary). He earned his doctorate at the University of Halle in Germany. He also studied under Abraham Kuyper and Herman Bavinck at the Free University of Amsterdam. But his teaching was suspect. He was charged with treating the books of the Old Testament simply as separate historical documents and of not doing justice to these books as formed by the Holy Spirit into an organic unity of truth. It was charged that he had been strongly influenced by the Higher Criticism of the Bible while studying in Germany. It was also averred that he stressed too much the

---

[7]Cited by L. Praamsma, *Let Christ Be King*, Paideia Press, c1985, p. 135. Praamsma answers such criticisms of Kuyper as follows: "But first we must emphasize as strongly as possible that he was as much a man of special grace as of common grace. It may be true that there was a shift in emphasis in a later period of his life, but from the very outset the necessity of God's special grace – acceptance by God as His child apart from any merit of one's own part – was fundamental to Kuyper's thinking. We may safely say that it remained the main concern throughout his life. In short, Kuyper was and remained a Reformed Christian to the end of his life." *Ibid*, p. 136.

[8]John Bolt, *Christian and Reformed Today*, Paideia Press, c1984, p. 48.

human element in the authorship of the Bible and did not do justice to the ruling divine factor.

In defense of himself and his teaching Janssen stated that he leaned heavily on the doctrine of common grace. After lengthy proceedings covering a number of years, unfortunately not unmarked by rancor, Janssen was deposed from his position. Persistent clamor for action coming from Janssen's colleagues at the school and throughout the church finally resulted in a thorough report by an investigating committee of the Curatorium (Board of Trustees). There were majority and minority reports of the committee's findings, with one report more favorable to Janssen's teaching than the other. But both reports agreed that the professor's teaching had no place in a Reformed seminary. On the basis of these findings the synod deposed Janssen in 1922.

Thus the Christian Reformed Church made clear that in its judgment the doctrine of common grace cannot be appealed to as warrant for a teaching that is not in harmony with basic beliefs of the church. Common grace, the chuch said in effect, cannot be looked upon as being some sort of free-floating divine beneficence that places a halo of acceptablility around every product of serious human thought and culture.

Then came 1924, when the church announced its three points in answer to those in the church who denied common grace; and when the church called for further study of the doctrine, a call to which there was little positive response. Plainly understanding of this teaching calls for further reflection. The vagueness that surrounds the subject cannot be helpful in the pursuit of our full Christian calling and witness.

Some Observations and Suggestions

In the hope that some small contribution may be made to further reflection I here offer some observations and suggestions so that perhaps a tiny step might be taken toward better understanding of the rich truth that is expressed by the term common grace.

1. What about the term *common grace*? Recently John Bolt has said that "the term 'common grace,' as its critics have eloquently argued, is indeed poorly chosen. The term 'grace'

should be limited to the sphere of redemption."[9] Others have shared that opinion. It was interesting to note that a minister who shared Bolt's objection to the term common grace had to agree with me when I observed that what we speak of as "common grace" is indeed gracious in character, by whatever name we may call it. However, this objection is a weighty one and deserves careful consideration. Perhaps this very objection may point to a line of approach to the matter that may not only undercut the objection somewhat, but may also help us to think more scripturally about the question.

2. To speak of grace is to speak of sin. Grace by its very nature implies sin as a reality in human experience and history. When sin entered human history, as recorded in Genesis 3, it brought dire consequences. It brought a curse on the sinner and on the world. To one of his creatures God said, "Cursed are you above all livestock and all the wild animals." To man God said, "cursed is the ground because of you." The only relief from the curse is in grace, the grace of God who made all and rules all.

   Was relief from the curse brought about by some general attitude of grace toward all of God's creation? Not at all. Relief came through a specific pronouncement by God. God said that one born of woman would come to destroy the evil one and his works. In other words, grace in relief of the curse of sin came when God's historical program of redemption was instituted. There was not then nor could there ever be relief from sin and its curse apart from the saving work of God's only Son.

3. In this connection we must take note of those may passages in Scripture which set forth Christ's saving work in broad, cosmic terms. God is always Lord of his creation. He has never deserted the creation which was "very good" in his eyes. He has sent forth his Son to be the redeemer of the world. Just as the effects of sin reach to all parts of God's creation, so the work of the Redeemer is cosmic in scope. He is described as the "true light that gives light to every man." These words of John 1:9 refer not just to Christ

---

[9] *Ibid.*

as the creating Word. These words refer to that glorious being as he came in our flesh for God's redemptive purposes; he "came from the Father, full of grace and truth," the one introduced by John the Baptist, who came as a witness to "testify concerning that light, so that through him all men might believe." In a context in which the apostle Paul deprecates human wisdom as folly he writes to the Corinthian Christians, "All things are yours . . . and you are of Christ, and Christ is of God" (I Cor. 3:21-23).

To the Ephesians Paul wrote that "God placed all things under his (Christ's) feet and appointed him head over everything for the church which is his body, the fullness of him who fills everything in every way" (Eph. 1:22). He wrote as follows to the Colossians: "And he (Christ) is the head of the body, the church; he is the beginning and the firstborn among the dead, so that in everything he might have the supremacy. For God was pleased to have all his fullness dwell in him, and through him to reconcile to himself all things, whether things on earth or things in heaven, by making peace through his blood, shed on the cross" (Col. 1:18-20). Also elsewhere Paul relates the saving work of Christ to a broader goal than the salvation of the elect when he writes to Timothy that God "is the Savior of all men, and especially of those who believe" (I Tim. 4:10).

From these passages it is clear that God's intent with the redemptive work of the Messiah is to spread blessings that go beyond the specific goal of redeeming God's own, those who believe, the elect. This sin-cursed world is the object of God's love, the love that sent the Savior into the world, as John 3:16 clearly states. Those whom Christ saves are the salt of the earth and the light of the world. That savor must affect all of life and that light must shine everywhere. Witness to God's renewing grace in Christ must be carried to all peoples so that all mankind shall be invited to share in the riches of that grace. God is "good to all; he has compassion on all he has made" (Ps. 145:8). Jesus taught us, "Love your enemies and pray for those who persecute you, that you may be sons of your Father in heaven. He causes his sun to rise on the evil and the good, and sends rain on the righteous and the unrighteous" (Matt. 5:44-45). The psalm that carries the repeated refrain "His love endures forever" celebrates God's works of creation and redemption, and contains in its conclusion these words, "and who gives food to every creature. His love endures forever" (Ps. 136).

4. The God who made all things and found delight in them as the morning stars sang together is the same God who sent his only Son to redeem the world so that the song of the Lamb might resound throughout heaven. The Creator's redeeming work envisions a new heaven and a new earth. "The creation waits in eager expectation for the sons of God to be revealed. For the creation was subjected to frustration, not by its own choice, but by the will of the one who subjected it, in hope that the creation itself will be liberated from its bondage to decay and brought into the glorious freedom of the children of God. We know that the whole creation has been groaning as in the pains of childbirth right up to the present time. Not only so, but we ourselves, who have the firstfruits of the Spirit, groan inwardly as we wait eagerly for adoption of sons" (Rom. 8:19-23).

5. There is throughout Scripture an evident intertwining of concepts relating to creation and redemption, to nature and to grace. Therefore we are not thinking scripturally when we set up a false disjunction between nature and grace, between God's redeeming love in Christ and his beneficence toward all his created works. Such disjunction is bound to lead to notions of common grace that are too general, notions that cut the conception of common grace loose from the redemptive purposes of God. Hence we have trouble with Bavinck's teaching that in Old Testament times grace was divided, with common grace and special grace each flowing in its own stream bed. This comment is made with special reference to history after Noah. The covenant with Noah is often referred to as the covenant of nature or the covenant of common grace. It is preferable to follow those who teach that this covenant is "most intimately connected" with the covenant of grace.[10] On the other hand Bavinck is surely correct when he says that Christ did not come

---

[10]See L. Berkhof, *Systematic Theology*, Wm. B. Eerdmans Publishing Co., Grand Rapids, 1949. Pp. 294ff.

as Savior just to restore the ethical-religious life of man, leaving all else undisturbed, as if all else has not been damaged by sin and so was not in need of restoration. Christ's restorative work reaches as far as sin reaches, says Bavinck. But this solid theologian seems to have been carried away when he exclaims that "Just as far as sin reaches so far the love of the Father and the grace of the Son and the communion of the Holy Spirit stretches over all."[11] This benediction belongs to special grace; it was pronounced by the apostle Paul upon the church at Corinth (II Cor. 13:14). False disjunctions between special grace and common grace are to be rejected, as pointed out earlier, but this does not mean that there are no very real distinctions between them.

Contextual Grace

6. In the light of the above comments I would like to make a suggestion, namely, that we think of that which we call common grace as "contextual grace." Students of the Bible are quite aware of the interlocking relationship that exists between a text and its context, a context that may be thought of as the verses contiguous to the text or more broadly as a section of the Bible or the Bible as a whole. Readers familiar with recent developments in missiology will relate the suggestion being made here to the concept of contextualization in the presentation of the gospel in different cultures.[12]

7. The term *contextual* clearly establishes a very real connection between common grace and special grace, that is, God's saving grace in Jesus Christ. The term prohibits the emergence of all loose and vague notions of common grace as a kind of free-floating divine beneficence that does not do justice to the grim reality of the sinfulness that has

---

[11]H. Bavinck, *De Algemeene Genade.* Address given in 1894. Grand Rapids, Eerdmans-Sevensma, pp. 26-28.

[12]See Harvie M. Conn, "The Missionary Task Of Theology: A Love/Hate Relationship." Address given on the occasion of Conn's inauguration as Professor of Missions at Westminster Theological Seminary. *Westminster Theological Journal,* Spring 1983.

affected man and all his works. Likewise the term protects us from losing sight of the antithesis between that which is redeemed and that which is not, between men who are regenerate and men who are not, between the church and the world. Notions of common grace that are not oriented to the antithesis do injustice to the very idea of grace.

8. The term contextual points to the centrality of God's redeeming purpose in history and to the supreme delight which God has in his redeemed people, his church, the apple of his eye. The term is, therefore, in full harmony with A. Kuyper's opening declaration in the Foreword to his opus on common grace, in which he states that the solid and set starting-point for all discussion around the subject of common grace is that *grace is particular*. Nothing may set aside or compromise this "middelpunt" of our Reformed confession. John Murray makes the same point when he says, "The redemptive purpose of God lies at the very centre of this world's history. While it is not the only purpose being fulfilled in history and while it is not the one purpose to which all others may be subordinated, yet it is surely the central stream of history. It is however in the wider context of history that the redemptive purpose of God is realized. This wider context we have already found to be a dispensation of divine forbearance and goodness. In other words, it is that sphere of life or broad stream of history provided by common grace that provides the sphere of operation for God's special purpose of redemption and salvation."[13] Attention is called to Professor Murray's use of the word *context* in this citation.

9. Kuyper gives us a good illustration of common grace as contextual grace in the *pax Romana* that prevailed at the time of the birth of Christ and succeeding years.[14] God in his wise and gracious providence so directed world history so that when Christ came in the fullness of time much of the world was under the control of one great power, and

---

[13]*Collected Writings of John Murray*, Vol. II. The Banner of Truth Trust, c1977, p. 113.

[14]*De Gemeene Gratie II*, pp. 165-187.

one dominant language was the means of human communication. So Christ's ambassadors could carry the gospel throughout the Mediterranean world with benefit of the rule of Rome and its citizenship, and with benefit of one language crossing all boundaries. By his common grace God made good preparation for the forward march of the work of his special grace, the church of Jesus Christ. So God's special grace could carry on within the context of his common grace.

10. The appropriateness of the term *contextual grace* is apparent in A. Kuyper's discussion of "Common Grace and Science and Art." After making the characteristically Kuyperian observation that "the life of particular grace does not stand by itself, but is by God placed in the midst of the life of common grace," the Amsterdam theologian goes on to make plain that science (*Wetenschap*), which belongs to the area (*erf*) of common grace, is bound to develop into an unbearable materialistic and atheistic body of knowledge if left to itself. Such increasingly bold unbelief forces Christendom to see that it must develop an educational program on the basis of "her own principles," a program which "knows the mystery of all wisdom and knowledge in Christ."[15]

It is much the same in Kuyper's discussion of common grace and art. Art belongs to the domain (*erf*) of common grace. But then Kuyper goes into an extended commentary on the necessity of rescuing art from a natural tendency to moral and even technical decadence. In other words, Christians must express their faith and life-style in art. If they do not do this art will degenerate more and more by separating the holy and the natural from each other. Thus Kuyper argues that art, which operates in the area of common grace, needs the moral and spiritual illumination furnished by special grace in order to produce objects of art that are truly beautiful. In the areas of science and

---

[15]*De Gemeene Gratie* III, pp. 37-43. Kuyper's essay on "Common Grace and Science and Art" is the last section in Volume III of his great work on common grace. This significant chapter is not without some questionable argumentation, though such is not crucial to his main discussion.

art common grace is contextual grace, with special grace at the center of that broad vision that encompasses all of life, culture and history. The pertinence of Kuyper's line of thought here is especially evident when we consider what is produced today in hard rock music. Both the words of the lyrics sung and the sound of the music are commonly far removed from what might be called beautiful and much closer to what we would call unattractive or ugly or even hideous.

11. This brings us to a final comment under "Some Observations and Suggestions." Common grace is contextual to special grace. All grace is God's wondrous response to sin, to violation of the moral standards of his law. God's ethical demands on human life are never relaxed or reduced. All human life is under the scrutiny and judgment of God's holy law. The person who lives by God's special grace in Christ has no fear of that scrutiny or judgment because by faith he is bound to Christ, who took that judgment upon himself for those who are his. And the Christian can stand the scrutiny of that law because he is risen with Christ unto a new life in which God's law is a delight and not a threat or burden. The person who is not a beneficiary of that special grace in Christ cannot avoid the scrutiny and judgment of God's holy law. He and his works, his cultural products, must be tested by God's holy standards for human life. He may "do by nature things required by the law" (Rom. 2:14). He may find some pleasant relief from the rule of sin in his life due to the restraint of sin wrought by common grace and because of the "civic righteousness" he may be enabled to perform. Mankind's cultural products may give evidence of such benefits from common grace. But apart from special grace the scrutiny and judgment of God's law abide on those who have not found their treasure in the heaven-sent Savior and Lord of all of life. God's ethical framework for the life of his responsible image-bearer always stands. It may never be ignored or compromised.

Conclusion

We now return briefly to the two illustrations with which this essay began. Can we see common grace in the blasphemous play? Can we see common grace in the atheistic theory of evolution? Yes, in carefully defined ways, we can. We can see God's common grace in the capacities for creative writing and intellectual performance with which he endows people. The God who gave gifts for cultural production to the line of Cain still gives such gifts to mankind generally, also to those who may not use those gifts for God's glory. We can see God's common grace in the continuity and dependablility of nature so that there are laws of genetics, for instance, that operate to bring about the birth of men and women who can make significant contributions to human culture. In other words, the presence of sin in the human race has not resulted in unrelieved chaos and decay, not even among those who are reprobate. Among all mankind, also among unbelievers, there are governmental order and social stability, making for conditions suitable for cultural productivity that brings luster and pleasure to human existence.

However, there are limits to what can be spoken of as evidences of common grace in such cultural products. The blasphemous play violated the third commandment forbidding the misuse of God's holy name. The atheistic theory of evolution violates the first commandment by making God irrelevant and meaningless in his world, and worshipping nature as God, a god producing human beings by a process of natural selection and evolution through unknown and inconceivable eons of time. Therefore because such productions violate God's unchanging and irreducible moral laws, Christians cannot take such articles and make them part of their life of glorifying God in all things.

An illustration may help at this point. When I served as member of the Board of Trustees of Calvin College and Seminary in the seventies the president of the college told about an episode of confrontation with some students. A drama group on campus wanted to put on a play that carried much profanity. The president told the students that they could not make a public production of the play unless they substituted other harmless expressions in those places where God's name was misused. They students balked, saying that such tampering violated the integrity of the play. Though acknowledging that their point had some validity, the president held his ground. He indicated that he had no objection to the study of the play in class as a piece of literature with a qualified instructor in charge, but they could not take the blasphemous play and make it their own production and a production of the Christian college.

* * * * * * * *

Is Henry Vander Goot correct when he says that the "Mind of Common Grace has become the dominant mind" of the leadership of the Christian Reformed Church? Maybe he is correct. He is part of the church's academic community and therefore has insider insight that many of us do not have.

But what constitutes this "Mind of Common Grace?" Is this "mind" one which holds to a clear, well-defined conception of common grace? Does this mind work with the understanding that a valid formulation of the doctrine of common grace must include the antithesis in that very formulation? Or is this mind one that embraces a vague, ill-defined notion of common grace, a notion more assumed than understood? It seems that the latter is the case, in light of the failure of the church to move measurably beyond the sketchy three points of 1924.

Has this unfinished business meant impoverishment of the church? It seems impossible to think otherwise. Such impoverishment cannot fail to occur when a significant element of the faith is left dangling. Vague, ill-considered notions of the doctrine can be expected to appear. Furthermore, if a significant element of doctrine is left dangling in this way, what is the effect on the overall allegiance to the Reformed faith? The effect can hardly be anything other than a slippage of interest in and allegiance to the faith in other respects. An astute churchman like R. B. Kuiper observed in 1959, "Perhaps the most serious weakness of the Christian Reformed Church at present is a dearth of doctrinal discernment."[16] More recently another qualified student of the church has said, "Many Christians simply view the plethora of ecclesial traditions and church denominations as a kind of smorgasbord in which personal preference

---

[16]R. B. Kuiper, *To Be Or No To Be Reformed*, Zondervan Publishing House, Grand Rapids, 1959. P. 147.

and taste are the order of the day. Concern about the truth of doctrine or confession seems waning."[17] It cannot be denied that there is a general impatience with doctrinal discussions. Has the unfinished business we have been talking about contributed to this state of affairs in the church?

Surely questions such as these must be asked as we reflect on this unfinished business. Much time has elapsed since 1924. We have been busy with many things since then. We have left a weighty matter undone, to our hurt.

---

[17]John Bolt, *Christian and Reformed Today*, pp. 23f.

CHAPTER 3
1952—Watershed

In the year 1952 the Christian Reformed Church experienced what might be called an earthquake. It surely was a major shakeup, with the epicenter in Grand Rapids, Michigan, and the shock felt wherever there was a Christian Reformed presence. Aftershocks were felt for a long time afterward.

What happened in 1952? In that year Calvin Theological Seminary lost almost its entire faculty. By action of synod four professors were dismissed. Two others were granted emeritation for reasons of health. Another professor came very close to being dismissed, but he was spared and escaped with an admonition. He, Professor of Old Testament, was the only regular faculty member remaining on the staff. One other instructor was retained for special teaching services. So in 1952 the church's training school for preachers was almost wiped out. This drastic shakeup had a profound effect on the church at the vital center where its future leaders were trained. A case can be made for the contention that the year 1952 constituted a kind of watershed in the Christian Reformed Church, a watershed separating the seminary that had been from the seminary that would develop after 1952.

There is no point in discussing at some length the factors that made up the "Seminary situation" which was dealt with so drastically at that time. The situation was complex. Synod's advisory committee in the matter declared that the problem was "first of all one of intra-faculty relations . . . a violent clash between men" (*Acts of Synod 1952*, p. 97). The account of the Synod's handling of the explosive situation indicates no awareness of any doctrinal differences among the feuding faculty members. People who were present at the Synod of 1952, among them some who were very much involved in the action, disclose their feeling that there was more involved than a clash of personalities, but such more substantive factors could not be brought out in the lengthy and trying struggle at synod.

Nothing would be gained by trying to enter into a critical evaluation of what was done at the Synod of 1952. Such an effort at this late date would have to be regarded as presumptuous. However, one comment seems in order. As one reflects on the radical surgery that synod resorted to in seeking to resolve the "Seminary situation," one has to wonder how such sharp discord among mature Christian men could possibly be fully described as a clash among personalities. After all, they were not a group of wrangling kids who just couldn't get along.

An element contributing to the problem at the school was the presence of two contrary attitudes among the students. Many of the students had served in World War II. Some of these men returned from their military experience with a strong conviction that the Christian Reformed Church should move out of its status as a sheltered enclave and become more open to new ideas and attitudes. Others who returned from the war came to school with an equally strong conviction that in the world's turmoil and upheaval the Christian Reformed Church should hold fast to its principles and that any dilution of them would be perilous. The polarity between these two mindsets among the students added to the tensions making up the "Seminary situation."

A final comment on the problem dealt with in 1952 is one that careful students of the Christian Reformed Church and its institutions may well ponder. In their "Statement of the Problem" the advisory committee of the Synod said this, "Tensions and difficulties of a serious nature have existed for some time and it is quite probable that if remedial measures had been taken earlier the situation would not have assumed such serious proportions as have now become manifest. If the Board had taken more incisive action when the problem first came to their attention much of what is plaguing us today might have been averted" (*Acts of Synod 1952*, p. 97).

Setting Up A New Conflict

As the Synod of 1952 sought to lay to rest a troublesome conflict by the radical surgery it performed on the seminary faculty, the Synod, all unknowingly, laid the groundwork for another conflict.

This came about through the appointments the Synod made of new faculty members. Appointments were extended to able men, among them G. C. Berkouwer of the Netherlands and N. B. Stonehouse of Westminster Theological Seminary. Both of these men declined. Accepting appointments were John H. Kromminga (Church History), R. B. Kuiper (Practical Theology,) and Henry Stob (Apologetics and Ethics). Kuiper, who had just retired after long service at Westminster, most of the time as Chairman of the Faculty, became president of Calvin Seminary in those troubled times. He served until he retired in 1956.

While Kuiper was at the head of Calvin Seminary he was the dominant voice. But in time, for reasons of seniority, tenure, position and ability, the other two appointees in 1952 became in the view of many the two most influential figures in the Christian Reformed Church. John H. Kromminga succeeded Kuiper as president of the seminary in 1956 and held that important post for twenty-five years. Henry Stob, it appears, developed into the most effective and popular teacher on the faculty. In speaking of influential men the reference is to the role these men played in the councils and affairs of the church and in the training of its leadership. If one thinks of broader influence exerted also beyond the bounds of the Christian Reformed Church, then the names of Peter H. Eldersveld and Joel H. Nederhood of the Back to God Hour move to or near the top of the list.

The differences between Kromminga and Stob on the one hand and Kuiper on the other did not break out into open conflict, the kind of conflict that faced the church in 1952. The tension remained largely hidden from view. But it was nonetheless very real.

The key to the new division in the faculty can best be found in R. B. Kuiper's set of requirements for men who would teach in a Reformed theological seminary. He spelled out his set of qualifications to the Board of Trustees and also laid them out before the church in an article appearing in *The Banner* of May 15, 1953. Of supreme importance to Kuiper was the requirement that those who taught the future ministers of the church "must be thoroughly sound in doctrine. But that is not enough. No man may be permitted to teach at Calvin Seminary who does not possess a consuming zeal for the Reformed faith ... He must be truly militant in his defense of the Reformed faith against heresy."

It was no secret at the time that Kuiper was opposed to having either of these two men succeed him in the office of president of the seminary.[1] On what grounds did he oppose them? Because they did not, in his view, meet the standard for seminary professors which in the preceding paragraph we have called the key to the new conflict in the seminary. It is to be noted that Kuiper arrived at this judgment after serving side by side with these men on the seminary faculty.

This disagreement among these three leaders in the church is not to be dismissed as a passing family quarrel. It bears on the character of the seminary that emerged after 1952, especially after Kuiper retired in 1956. In assessing this difference between Kuiper and the other two professors something of importance has to be borne in mind. Kuiper had the confidence of the Christian Reformed Church, a confidence gained over many years. He had been one of the church's leading pulpiteers. He had served the church with distinction as president of Calvin College. And when the church wanted a trusted and competent leader at the time of the turmoil in 1952, R. B. Kuiper was sought out to give stability and direction at a time when such were sorely needed.

To the list of this man's credentials must be added the fact that he had experienced the complete confidence of some of the leading biblical and Reformed scholars of the twentieth century. I refer to J. Gresham Machen, C. Van Til, John Murray and E. J. Young.

Members of the Christian Reformed Church should ponder the fact that this man with such impressive credentials had serious misgivings regarding the strong commitment of these two men to the aggressive propagation and defense of the Reformed faith, these two men who would exercise signal leadership in the church for many years. What were the implications of this sharp difference for the future of the seminary and the church? The depth of Kuiper's feelings on this score was revealed at the Synod of 1959 when he made a critical speech opposing the appointment of the Professor of Apologetics to an "indefinite term."

----

[1] Clear evidence of Kuiper's feelings on this score can be found among his papers, now housed in the archives of Heritage Hall in the Library of Calvin College and Seminary.

The Winds Of Change

That changes were in the making in the character of the seminary became evident in a significant series of articles written by Henry Stob in connection with the denomination's observance of its centennial in 1957. The articles on the theme "The Mind of the Church" appeared in the *Reformed Journal* from March 1957 to September 1961, and were later included in a book of Stob's writings entitled *Theological Reflections*. These articles, when read and reread, give a clear signal that the future preachers of the church were under instruction whose spirit was markedly different from that which had characterized the school for many years prior to 1952. A few comments are therefore in order.

The professor saw three different minds or attitudes or perspectives in the church, two of them negative, according to the writer, and one positive. These "minds" were seen primarily as describing the relation of the Christian to the world. The two minds of negativity were labeled "the mind of safety" and "the militant mind." The third mind (presumably the professor's own mind as opposed to the other two) was called simply "the positive mind." These three minds are "not to be allocated to three distinct groups or "parties'," said the professor. "These three minds are in us all." Yet, though that had been said, the writer went on to say that "none of us is really able in the long run to endorse all three of these minds. As 'minds,' i.e., as 'total outlooks' or 'governing perspectives,' they exclude each other, and one of them must eventually be chosen and seated as king. Personal wholeness and integrity demand this choice" (*Reformed Journal*, Mar. 1957, pp. 4-5).

Such reductionism (one of the professor's favorite words in criticizing the two minds he rejected) cannot be left unchallenged. Such a declaration allows for the placing of those we disagree with into neatly defined categories that cannot accommodate the complex character of human attitudes. The varieties of attitude embraced by people are as diverse and multicolored as the individualities of these people. Herman Hoeksema, H. J. Kuiper, Clarence Bouma, C. Van Til, J. Gresham Machen and R. B. Kuiper could all be described as being militant in their defense and propagation of the faith. Yet, their attitudes toward the culture of the world were quite diverse. They cannot all be placed in one box on which are scribbled words like dogmatist, assault, warlike, fear, lovelessness, anti-cultural, humorless, etc. Such generalized characterizations are as unfair as they are unrealistic.

The professor's discussion of love and its commanding role in the exercise of "the positive mind" was off balance. Note well the following citation.

> Sin and evil as abstract entities remain fair game throughout all time; but since God struck at Himself on Golgotha all blows struck by men at other men are irrelevant and proscribed. The battle joined in Christ precludes all further battles, except such as may be permitted by special authorization to the ministers of the state. In the sphere of morals and religion there is for sinners one message only: that God is appeased and at war no more. What is therefore proper to God's messengers are beckonings, invitations, overtures to fellowship; and what they are called to are acts of healing, restoration, and reconstruction. It is this that the Positive Mind affirms in the face of Militancy, and in affirming it it believes itself fixed at the center of the Gospel. (*Reformed Journal*, March 1961, p. 8).

Could the professor possibly have been serious here? Do we as Christians fight against sin and evil as "abstract entities?" Do we not fight them as they come to expression in events and the deeds of men? In urging his readers "to contend for the faith" Jude was not speaking of sin and evil in the abstract; he was speaking of "certain men" who had "slipped in among you," men subject to "condemnation." Did not Paul say that he "fought wild beasts in Ephesus?" (I Cor. 15:32). Commentators are generally agreed that these "wild beasts" were human enemies of Paul's ministry. And today, do we not applaud the Rev. Don Wildmon of the American Family Association in his dogged fight against the merchants of obscenity and pornography?

Since God's saving work on Calvary, is "God appeased and at war no more?" Did not our Lord say that he "did not come to bring peace, but a sword?" Can one read the book of Revelation and conclude that God is "at war no more?" What about the seven bowls of God's wrath of Revelation 16? Then there is the one who rides the white horse; his name is Faithful and True, and "with justice he judges and makes war" (Rev. 19:11).

The Militant Mind

In the series of articles on the "minds" in the church most attention was given to criticism of the militant mind. Three articles were devoted to this mind whereas only one article dealt with the mind of safety and one with the positive mind.

Let it be said at once that every person who contends earnestly for the faith can benefit from reading what Dr. Strob had to say on the subject of militancy in the church. Certainly the aggressive defender and propagator of the faith is well warned, for example, that he refrain from being absolutistic about matters that may well be spoken of as mere opinion.

That the kind of thinking expressed in these articles on the "minds" in the church was influential can hardly be questioned. A few years after the appearance of these articles another series about the Christian Reformed Church broke into print under the heading "What Is Happening To Us?" This extended series was written by the Rev. Clarence Boomsma, a leading minister in the church who was pastor of the congregation of which Professor Stob was a member. The later series of articles, running in *The Banner* from January 1973 to the spring of 1975 (with some long interruptions) was instructive and worthwhile on many counts. Significantly the author of this later series adopted the same stance toward the mind of "militant orthodoxy" that the earlier series had set forth. Boomsma described militant orthodoxy as "a mentality of . . . conflict and antagonism," a "divisive movement" prompted by fear (*The Banner*, Mar. 28, 1975, p. 15). The author opined gratuitously that "the rule of fear in militant orthodoxy is quite easily and generally recognized." Equally gratuitous was the observation that this fear evidenced "lack of faith" (*The Banner*, April 11, 1975, p. 12.).

This kind of thinking in the seminary and in the church must be evaluated in the light of an obvious and important fact of our history. To promote a "positive" mind as the professor defined it as the true Christian mind over against the mind of militant orthodoxy is to contradict flatly a history which in its longer and broader frame includes names of leading figures like St. Paul, Polycarp, Athanasius, Irenaeus, Martin Luther, Guillaume Farel, John Calvin, John Huss, John Wycliffe, John Knox, Guido de Bres, Hendrick De Cock, H. P. Scholte, Abraham Kuyper, K. Vanden Bosch and Gysbert Haan. Every one of these men faithfully and aggressively promoted the true Christian faith against all sorts of errors. Though they promoted and defended the faith in different historical and cultural settings with their fine relativities, the plain fact is that all of them, and many more, had the mind of militant orthodoxy. Without their devoted efforts and struggles there would be no Christian Reformed Church for professors and preachers to write about.

What has to be the result when such thinking influences the future preachers in their training and when such attitudes spread through the church? Such thinking, so much out of step with our special history, can only make for confusion, uncertainty, and lack of clear-minded commitment to the faith we profess.

"Our Reformed character and commitment is perhaps not held with the same vigorous loyalty, nor championed with the same passion, nor emphasized so acutely in the whole range of church teaching as was true forty years ago." These words were spoken by Clarence Boomsma in an address he delivered in 1983, an address in which he maintained that "the Christian Reformed Church has remained theologically a *Reformed* orthodox church." In the same speech he said that "though the Christian Reformed Church remains staunchly orthodox in its theology, in spirit and in practice there has been . . . a loss of vigor and devotion in the defense and appreciation of the distinctively Reformed tenets of our faith." The speech again made use of Stob's three "minds" in the church and spoke critically (though mildly this time) of the militant mind. There was a curious irony in the references to the militant mind at work in the church in a speech that lamented decay in zeal for the faith. And there was another irony in this speech. The address was delivered on the occasion of the retirement of the president of Calvin Seminary after twenty-five years of service. Surely this position, more than any other in the church and occupied for a quarter century, offered the incumbent great opportunity to influence the theological health of the church. On this special occasion the speaker lamented "a loss of vigor and devotion in the defense and appreciation of the distinctively Reformed tenets of our faith." Was not just such a development what R. B. Kuiper had in view when he called for men who "possess a consuming zeal for the Reformed faith?" (Boomsma's address,

30

entitled "What Has Happened Theologically To The Christian Reformed Church Since World War II?," was published in the *Calvin Theological Journal* of April 1984, pp. 32-49).

More Evidence of the Watershed

There were further indications of significant change in the seminary following the watershed of 1952. An important piece of such evidence appeared in 1959. A student had written a series of articles in a student publication on the subject of Biblical Infallibility. The series started with an article entitled "Infallibility Questioned" (*Stromata*, Sept. 1958) and continued to the January issue of the magazine.

The articles caused a considerable stir in the church and also division among the members of the seminary faculty. The president of the seminary sought to calm the troubled waters by producing a paper entitled "How Shall We Understand 'Infallibility'?" The matter came before the Board of Trustees of Calvin College and Seminary. One faculty member (M. J. Wyngaarden, Professor of Old Testament and the only remaining member of the faculty from pre-watershed days) was not satisfied with the Board's decision in the matter and came to the Synod of 1959 with a Protest and Appeal. The critical point in the Protest and Appeal was the document written by the president of the seminary.

In his paper the president argued that the question facing the church was "what was believed to be infallible, and how far infallibility extended." He also said, "Granting that the Holy Spirit infallibly conveyed what He intended to teach, how shall we interpret Scriptural items which are on the periphery of that teaching?" Wyngaarden contended that at several points the president's paper was out of line with the Belgic Confession, especially Article V, in which the church confesses its faith as "believing without any doubt all things contained in" the Scriptures.

The account of the Synod's protracted discussion reveals that the contentions of the protestant were not sustained on all points. However, it is correct to conclude that in effect the protest was sustained on several counts. The Synod found the document written by the president to be ambiguous at some points, that he admitted his paper was in error on at least one point, and that he had revised his understanding of the

31

Confession at another point. It would have been well for the president to remember something he once wrote about the outcome of an earlier doctrinal controversy, namely, "It became apparent that the Christian Reformed Church was not willing to have the slightest doubt cast upon the infallibility of the Bible." (See John Kromminga, *The Christian Reformed Church — A Study in Orthodoxy*, 1949, p. 79).

Of God's Love and Hate

Further evidence of change at the seminary after the watershed of 1952 appeared in prolonged debate precipitated by an article written by the Professor of Missions in 1962. The article was entitled "God So Loved — All Men" (*Reformed Journal*, Dec. 1962). The article touched on sensitive and significant questions in Reformed theology. As the debate continued over a period of some five years, it became apparent that the writing of the professor lacked the clarity and precision that would be expected from one teaching in a seminary committed to the Reformed faith. Though the brother had written out of commendable concern for the missionary work of the church, his writings, including further articles on the subject, raised many questions regarding his understanding of the special love of God for his elect and his understanding of the efficacy of God's sovereign redeeming grace. At an adjourned meeting of the Synod of 1967 held in August it was decided to "admonish Professor Dekker for the ambiguous and abstract way in which he has expressed himself in his writing on the love of God and the atonement" (*Acts of Synod 1967*, p. 736).

The prolonged and intense discussion on the love of God prompted some writing on God's "hate." In the *Reformed Journal* of February 1963 an article appeared on the question "Does God Hate Some Men?" It was written by the Professor of Apologetics at Calvin Seminary. It has already been noted that R. B. Kuiper did not have full confidence in the thinking of the professor. Kuiper gave expression to some of his sharpest criticism in commenting on the following assertion in the article: "I think that to ascribe hate of persons to God is to pervert the very thought of God. I believe that we are emphatically not permitted by the total evidence of the Scriptures to say that God hates men in any distinct and significant meaning of the term."

Kuiper charged that such writing was contrary to the plain teaching of Scripture (Mal. 1:3, Rom. 9:13, Ps. 11:5, Ps. 5:5), and that there was "a strain of rationalism" in the professor's interpretation of the Bible. (See Heerema, *RB A Prophet In The Land,* pp. 193f).

* * * * *

Enough has been written to demonstrate that there was a new leadership in the church in the aftermath of the watershed of 1952. Further evidence of such change could be adduced by reference to two highly important documents bearing the number 44. But that is farther down the road and discussion of this material is reserved for the next chapters.

CHAPTER 4
44—A Stumbling Church

In the early seventies two documents appeared in the Christian Reformed Church which did not prove to be a blessing to this part of the body of Christ. Rather than sharpen the church's sense of itself and its witness, these documents served rather to befog the church's vision. Both of these documents, or committee reports, bore the identification number 44 in the *Acts of Synod*. In this chapter and the following one we deal with each of these productions, calling the first 44-1972 and the second 44-1973.

Much has been said and written about these documents, so much so that even a bare mention of them tends to induce a yawn. I am quite aware of this fact, and shall therefore strive to be pointed in my comments.

Before entering into the discussion of these significant reports two facts about both must be recalled in our assessment of these papers. The first fact is that both documents appeared at earlier synods and both were returned to their respective study committees for clarification. The second fact is that even after these reports came before succeeding synods in revised form, the synods of 1972 and 1973 determined that introductory clarifying "points" and "observations" had to be added in order to make the fruits of the studies presentable to the churches.

44-1972—The Bible's Authority

Early on in the discussion at Synod 1972 of Report 44 on "The Nature and Extent of Biblical Authority" a delegate to the assembly spoke in the following vein:

There is much in this report with which we have to agree. Indeed, there is much that is very well stated in the matter of Biblical authority. It says, "The authority of the Bible is the authority of God himself." It also says, "We confess that the Bible is the inspired Word of God and that it is unconditionally authoritative for faith and life . . . The entire Scripture in its entirety, as the inspired Word of God, is authoritative." The report further says so well, "Thus what Scripture says, God says. The entire 'God-breathed' Scripture is the authoritative Word of God." And we rejoice in a statement like this, "The nature and extent of Scripture's authority can really be discovered only through a life of obedient submission to it, a life guided by the Holy Spirit." To all of that we can speak a hearty "Amen!"

However, there is another line of thought in this report that troubles me. Listen to these citations from the report. We read, "While the entire Scripture speaks with divine authority, this authority is understood correctly and specifically only when one takes account of what God said, how he spoke, to whom he spoke, etc." Again we read, "The Bible is a unique book and it has been inspired with a particular purpose in view. Unless one acknowledges that purpose and uses it as the key for understanding, even though he confesses the inspiration and authority of Scripture, he has not submitted himself to the real authority of Scripture." Please listen to one more sentence from the report. It says, "And when Christian interpreters, although confessing the full authority of Scripture and believing in Jesus Christ, derive from the Scripture teachings which do not reflect the intended meaning of Scripture, then they are not submitting to the authentic authority of the Word of God."

Brothers, do we really believe what these words are saying? I do not believe this. These words say to me that sincere Christians who love the Bible and the Savior it presents but who do not agree with us on all points of Biblical interpretation, do not honor the authority of the Scripture. Would I care or dare to say that to my conservative Baptist or Lutheran friends? If I should be so brazen as to suggest that to them, they could rightly become annoyed with me for accusing them falsely and for exhibiting arrogance.

Is it true that failure to comply with authority always means failure to recognize authority? A father, before leaving for his office in the morning, leaves instruction with his son to trim the hedges that day. When he returns home later in the day he sees that his son has not trimmed the hedges. He calls his son and asks him to explain his neglect of duty. "Dad," the son replied, "I thought you asked me to trim the edges of the lawn. See, I did that." Did the son in his misunderstanding of his father's order fail to honor the authority of his father? Obviously not. Failure to interpret correctly some writing or teaching or instruction does not therefore mean failure to honor the authority expressed in or by such writing, teaching or instruction.

Furthermore, these citations whose thrust I am questioning say to me that only the advanced Biblical scholar honors the real, authentic authority of the Word of God. I do not think we really believe that.

Brothers, this report, good as it is in many of the things it says, is seriously flawed on these counts. It is therefore unacceptable and should be rejected or revised.

After the above remarks were delivered speaker after speaker came back to the point in an effort to clear up the matter. As the long debate on 44-1972 drew to its close a delegate, one with a doctor's degree in theology, declared, "Rev. N . . .'s point has not been answered."

Has the point ever been answered? There have been many discussions held, many speeches made, and many articles written about this report on Biblical Authority, but to date I am not aware that the point has been answered. The problems with 44-1972 were highlighted by the fact that five years after synod dealt with the report in 1972, two Classes (groups of churches) came to synod with overtures asking for clarification. It is evident the report had not brought clarity to the churches but rather confusion on something so basic as the authority of the Bible.

Only the blindest critic would care to claim that the report had no virtues other than those mentioned in the early part of the remarks by the speaker at synod. There was also some cogent teaching about the relationship between biblical content and scientific findings. Science should not be regarded as dictating biblical interpretation (*Acts of Synod 1972*, pp. 513ff.). Also, out of the report came a fitting guideline warning that the "event character" of Biblical history should not be called into question. However, this point has not impressed everyone in the church with equal force. It is interesting to observe that the committee of the Board of Trustees of Calvin College and Seminary that investigated the evolutionary views of certain professors in 1987-88 had this to say, "We realize that what Synod meant by the phrase 'event character' isn't as clear as could be wished" (*Acts of Synod 1988*, p. 593).

37

The Flaw

What was the serious flaw that the speaker at Synod 1972 fingered? One hesitates to offer an answer to that question, for among the authors of 44-1972 were men whose theological insight and competence one has to respect. Yet the history of this report at Synod 1972 and in subsequent years calls for an answer.

I suggest that the flaw is this: the report, in the passages cited in the latter part of the speech recorded above, makes the reality of the authority of Scripture dependent on man's interpretation of Scripture. If one doesn't interpret some portion of Scripture in a certain way, then Scripture has no real authority for that person, no matter how earnestly he avows his submission to the Bible's authority.

To be sure, only truth is authoritative; falsehood has no actual authority. But where is that authority located? In man's understanding of the Bible? Is the Bible's authority contingent on man's thinking processes with all their limitations, meanderings and vagaries? Jesus said, "Your word is truth" (John 17:17). The authority of the Bible resides in the very truth of God's Word, and its reality, its authenticity, is in no way dependent on man's apprehension of the truth that is authoritative. Hence Synod 1972 spoke as follows: "Synod calls the churches to a wholehearted recognition that Scripture, which is the saving revelation of God in Jesus Christ, addresses us with full divine authority and that this authority applies to Scripture in its total extent and in all its parts" (*Acts of Synod 1972*, p. 68). This declaration by the Synod is fully in line with the words of the Belgic Confession, Article V, where the church gives expression to its faith regarding the Scriptures as "believing without any doubt all things contained in them, not so much because the church receives and approves them as such, but more especially because the Holy Spirit witnesses in our hearts that they are from God, and also because they carry the evidence thereof in themselves."

An elder at the synod of 1972 said it well when he asserted that the authority of any document is found in the signature to that document. How true! A letter telling me to appear in court at a certain time has no authority if it is signed by the neighbor who is suing me in a boundary dispute. But such a letter does have authority if it is signed by the sheriff or

38

by the clerk of the court. God the Holy Spirit is the author of the Bible and it is this divine authorship that invests the Bible with its authority. This authority resides in the Word written, and the reality of that authority is in no way contingent on my greater or lesser understanding of the contents of that Word.

Report 44-1972 at the point under discussion says plainly that the real authority of the Bible is not recognizable by one who does not have considerable expert knowledge of the Scripture. So only the expert in such matters can know the true authority of the Bible. Can the church of Christ tolerate such elitist thinking? What about the average conscientious church member who has had no advanced schooling in Bible studies and theology? What about the church member who may not know how some passage in Chronicles or Proverbs or Ezekiel fits in the redemptive purpose of Scripture? Is his sincere acknowledgement of the authority of the Bible to be regarded as little more than meaningless patter? A line of thought that leads in that direction demonstrates its own lack of cogency. It is a well known fact of church history that the sure belief of the plain people of the church in the authority of the Bible has been a source of strength and stability among God's people. The line of thought we are here challenging must lead us into the wastelands of relativism and subjectivism, something which the authors of the report would reject, to be sure. Yet, their writing at the point at issue must inevitably lead down that treacherous path.

Where Such Thinking Leads

Where such thinking leads becomes clear when we look at developments in the Reformed Churches in the Netherlands just a few years later. First let us recall that it was a request from these churches in the Netherlands (De Gereformeerde Kerken in Nederland) coming to the Christian Reformed Church by way of the Reformed Ecumenical Synod (now named Reformed Ecumenical Council) that led to the writing of Report 44 on "The Nature and Extent of Biblical Authority." The synod of 1969 appointed a committee to study "the nature and extent of Biblical authority, and in particular 'the connection between the content and purpose of Scriptures as the saving revelation of God in Jesus Christ and the *consequent and deducible authority of Scripture'* " (italics by EH). The words in italics should have alerted the church that treacherous waters were ahead, for these words say that the authority of Scripture is consequent upon and deducible from a certain formulation as to the intent of Scripture. In other words, the serious problem with Report 44-1972 which is being discussed here was already clearly present in the mandate given to the study committee appointed in 1969. These words in italics came from a letter addressed by De Gereformeerde Kerken in Nederland to the meeting of the Reformed Ecumenical Synod in 1968. (See *Acts of Synod 1969*, p. 102).

In the year 1980 the synod of De Gereformeerde Kerken in Nederland unanimously adopted its own report on the nature (*aard*) of Biblical authority. It was a result of a six-year study. This report was published separately under the title *God Met Ons*, translated *God With Us*.

It is significant that this report begins with a lengthy discussion of the nature of truth. This discussion is philosophical, not biblical. The nature of truth is not dealt with in the light of what the Bible says on the subject. The accent is on understanding truth in a world of change.

Of special importance in this document is the teaching that truth is *relational*. Truth must be seen in relation to man's changing needs and cultures. Truth is not absolute. It changes from age to age, from person to person.

We should not be surprised at certain things that come out in this report, adopted unanimously by the synod of a denomination with which the Christian Reformed Church has had such close ties. The inspiration of Scripture as understood by most Reformed theologians in the past is criticized as being mechanical, with the human authors of the Bible acting simply as "pencils in the hand of God." In fact, we are told that all of the great Reformed theologians were bound by their times. We today have to adapt to new ideas, new times. The gospel writers, the report contends, often put words into the mouth of Jesus that he never actually spoke. Miracles can be accepted, but one Christian can accept more of them, some less. As to the great miracle of Christ's resurrection, some church members may doubt its factuality. The church should be patient with such members, the report says.

Under the rule of the *relational* notion of truth there is no longer any sense in speaking of an inerrant and infallible Bible. The human element in the Bible is inseparable from the divine, so that we have a divine-human book in which human error comes through again and again. The Bible is no more reliable than any other human reporting of history. Also, there are different literary styles (genres) in Scripture, reflecting differing cultures, differing attitudes. So some of the accounts in the Bible must be taken as simple stories, sometimes highly imaginative ones. So there are, the report says, folk tales in the Bible, like the story of Jonah in the whale and the story of Lot's intercourse with his daughters.

This discussion of the Dutch report on the authority of Scripture with its *relational* idea of truth can be brought to a close with these observations. First of all, we must observe that this *relational* idea of truth and its authority is virtually identical with *relativism*, which means that there is no sure truth, but only a searching for truth in the changing times and attitudes and situations of peoples in the course of history. Secondly, this *relational* idea of truth reminds us of the notion of truth that has prevailed in dialectical theology (Barth, et al), namely, that truth is *encounter*. Barth has said that the Bible as such is not truth, but it becomes truth for us in the faith experience.

A fine and trustworthy Reformed scholar, the late Louis Praamsma, summarizes our evaluation of the report *God With Us* most aptly when he says that "the Word of God and the preaching of that Word is related to men and times. God spoke to His people of the old covenant in terms of the situation of that old covenant; and to His people of the new covenant in terms of the situation of that new one. The shadows of the old dispensation came to fulfillment in the new dispensation. The apostle Paul became a Jew to the Jews and a Greek to the Greeks. The missionaries to our old German forefathers spoke in the cultural environment of those Germans. The preachers in the time of war in the Netherlands spoke the language of an occupied country. The preachers in a concentration camp speak the language of that concentration camp. It would be simply foolish to deny all this. But the point is that God's truth does not depend on all these relationships but transcends them; that it does not *become* truth by human cooperation, but that God's Word *is* truth" (*The Outlook*, Nov. 1981, p.6).

Report 44 on Biblical Authority stumbled when it tried to define the "real" or "authentic" authority of the Bible in relation to man's understanding of the message of the Bible. The restless yearnings of the heart of sinful man find peace when he hears the authoritative voice of his God in the Word that saves, an authoritative voice that is both majestic and gracious. As he grows in his understanding of that redemptive Word he submits increasingly to that blessed authority that lovingly called him from darkness to light. But that authority does not depend on his understanding. Rather that authority feeds his understanding and undergirds it. Saul of Tarsus began to understand that redemptive Word when he was arrested by the authoritative voice of his Lord on the road to Damascus.

Report 44-1972 did not stumble as badly as the 1980 report entitled *God With Us*, but it was definitely on the same hazardous path. This path must inevitably lead to the loss of a Bible with actual moral and spiritual authority. The church that produced *God With Us* has taken a position on homosexuality that denies the authority of the Bible's teaching on the subject, subordinating that teaching to current psychological and sociological insights. The Christian Reformed Church with its report 44-1972 has been influenced in adopting its current position on women in office by the belief that certain teachings of the Bible on this score are bound to bygone attitudes and cultures, and are therefore no longer authoritative. Such are the results when the real authority, the essential authority, of the Bible is defined as being dependent on man's understanding of what the Bible says, with that understanding undergoing change from age to age, from culture to culture, from person to person. And among the people of the Word uncertainty and confusion grow.

CHAPTER 5
44-1973—
The Church Stumbles Again

More confusion and uncertainty were pumped into the church in 1973. Then the synod adopted certain guidelines for understanding the nature of ecclesiastical office and ordination, guidelines based on and growing out of an extensive report on the subject of "Ecclesiastical Office and Ordination." (See *Acts of Synod 1973*, pp. 61-64, 635-716).

Here was a report bearing signatures that indicated authorship by a blue ribbon committee. The members of this committee were four college professors of Bible, a seminary professor, the president of the seminary, and the Stated Clerk of the Christian Reformed Church. Almost all had doctor's degrees. Surely against such a formidable line-up one hesitates to say anything critical of report 44-1973.

Synod 1973 did not hesitate to speak critically of the report and of the Guidelines. It is well to recall that the synod of 1972 had sent the report back to the study committe because of certain lingering questions, especially about the matter of the authority of the special offices in the church. Synod 1973 was still not satisfied. The synod's advisory committee made this statement: "While your advisory committee is in general agreement with Report 44, it feels that the study committee has not presented a full and integrated statement on ecclesiastical office and ordination."

To demonstrate further its unease with the report and the Guidelines the synod adopted several "observations" to serve as a "framework within which the 'guidelines for understanding the nature of ecclesiastical office and ordination' are to be understood." The second "observation" declared that "nowhere in the New Testament is there a conflict between authority and service, or between ruling and love." Also the synod adopted the proposed Guidelines with some significant revisions recommended by the advisory committee.

What's The Problem?

The present writer would want to be the last to say that the report is without merit. Its emphasis on the servant character of church office commends itself. Again and again the report confronts us with the words of our Master, "I am among you as one who serves" (Luke 22:27). Any officebearer in the church should wish to thank the authors of the report for so strongly reminding him that his office is not a matter of status or prestige, but of humble service in Christ's name.

Would that our discussion of 44-1973 could be closed at this point. But it cannot be. The wholly proper thrust of the report regarding the servant character of church office is advanced at too great a cost. And this high cost makes the report just about useless as a worthy contribution to our understanding of office and ordination, and to our exercise in officebearing.

An illustration may help at this point. In a presidential election year in the United States Republicans might seek to promote their cause by claiming that all Democrats are blind communists, or Democrats might seek to promote their cause by charging that all Republicans are rigid, unthinking rightists.

The authors of 44-1973 have presented their idea of office in somewhat the same way, by presenting their concept of office over against a view that amounts to a caricature. They set up a false antithesis. It appears in the report's commentary on Hebrews 13:17, where the readers are admonished as follows, "Obey your leaders and submit to their authority. They keep watch over you as men who must give an account." Of the obedience here enjoined the report had this to say, "Christians ought to find such obedience and submission easy and natural, since they are in such situations submitting, not to authoritarian masters, but to faithful servants."

Note the heavily prejudiced word *authoritarian*; it signals the antithesis referred to above. Why the frequent occurrence of this word in 44-1973? Were the officebearers in the Christian Reformed Church acting in such a heavy-handed, authoritarian manner that synodical action was needed to correct such a condition? That is highly doubtful. Webster defines the word *authoritarian* thus: "of, relating to or favoring blind submission to authority . . . concentration of power in a leader or elite" group. One cannot help asking whether this report was significantly influenced by the anti-establishment, anti-authority spirit that swept across western society in the sixties and early seventies. Because this report worked with a false antithesis it is properly called a *tendentious* document. This word means "written or said with the aim of promoting a particular point of view." For this reason the report is marked by strained exegesis and also by some significant omissions. We proceed to note some examples of each.

Strained Exegesis

Man as God's image-bearer is given "dominion" ("rule" – NIV) over the rest of creation. The way man is to exercise his dominion is "spelled out," the report says, in the instruction he is given to "work . . . and care for" the Garden of Eden. Thus man "virtually becomes the servant of the 'lower creation,' " says the report. Does such teaching, with its obvious element of truth, get at the true character of man's God-assigned "dominion" or "rule" over the rest of creation?

Man's exercise of authority as described in the preceding paragraph should reflect the way God exercises his authority, man being God's image-bearer. "The Creator-Father is so concerned about the welfare of his creatures that he constantly serves them by providing them with food, water, clothing, and many other gifts . . . Divine authority, therefore is a serving authority" (*Acts of Synod 1973*, p. 692). True enough, but does this insight do justice to the authority of God? Is the sovereignty of the Almighty adequately described in such language?

The word for preacher in New Testament Greek is *keerux,* meaning herald. We find this word three times in the Greek New Testament. Even though the verb form of this word (*keerussein*) occurs much more frequently (61 times in the N.T.), the report makes some gratuitous observations about the limited use of the word *keerux*. "Why this infrequent usage?" the report asks, and then answers, "Probably because the word *keerux* was commonly used in Greek literature to describe a kind of elevated personage who was inviolable because he was under divine protection . . . The very infrequency of the word *keerux* in the New Testament, therefore, underscores the importance of the 'servant concept' underlying office in the New Testament (*ibid*, p. 662). Reading so much into the fact that *keerux* occurs only three times in the New Testament (even though *keerussein*

45

is used frequently) pinpoints the tendentious character of report 44-1973.

Such bending of the meaning of Scripture to support the position taken by the authors of report 44-1973 is apparent also in their handling of I Timothy 3:4-5. Here we read that a bishop (or elder) "must manage his own family well and see that his children obey him with proper respect. (If anyone does not know how to manage his own family, how can he take care of God's church?)" In commenting on this passage 44-1973 rejects an "authoritarian kind of domination" by the elders, as if that is seen as a proper exegetical option by any reasonable interpreter. Not only does 44-1973 call up this extreme interpretation in order to promote its special servant idea of office, the report also makes no comment on the second part of verse four, which requires the elders to "see that his children obey him with proper respect." I Timothy 3:4-5 certainly represents the office of elder as having real authority, though not the kind of authoritarian domination that 44-1973 constantly brings forth to reinforce its particular idea of servanthood in office.

The same kind of strained exegesis is evident in the interpretation of other relevant passages of Scripture. We mention two more passages here. In I Thessalonians 5:12 we read, "Now we ask you, brothers, to respect those who work hard among you, who are over you in the Lord and who admonish you." (See the report, p. 701). I Timothy 5:17 reads as follows, "The elders who direct the affairs of the church well are worthy of double honor, especially those who work in preaching and teaching." (See the report, p. 702).

Significant Omissions

Report 44-1973 is intent on presenting a picture of the New Testament church in terms of "the fluid New Testament situation with regard to office." Hence the fourth Guideline as presented to synod read as follows, "From the beginning these special ministries were functional in character, arising under the guidance of the Spirit primarily in the interests of good order and efficiency in the church, created as a means to the end of enabling the church to carry out Christ's work in the world most efficiently and effectively" (ibid, p. 715). In this connection it is illuminating to read the fourth observation which Synod 1973 adopted for the correct understanding of the

Guidelines. It reads as follows, "Because God is a God of order, and because the people of God are subject to many weaknesses and errors and in need of spiritual leadership in the face of a hostile world, Christ grants, by his Holy Spirit, gifts of ruling service and serving authority (service and authority) to particular people whom the church must recognize, in order that their gifts may be officially exercised for the benefit of all" (ibid, p. 62).

It is clear that the authors of 44-1973 wished to picture a loose, fluid situation in which, under the Holy Spirit, different functions came into action as need and occasion demanded. This view of the New Testament church scene cannot stand unchallenged when we consider the most important office in the New Testament church except for the office of apostle. That is the office of elder. Why did report 44-1973 not contain an in-depth study of the relationship between the office of elder in the New Testament church and the prominent place of elders in the Old Testament economy? One has to regard the absence of such a study as a glaring omission. In the ongoing life and work of the synagogue in the time of Christ and the apostles, elders played a prominent governing role in the "church" which nurtured them and which served in many ways as a model for the developing Christian church. The suggestion that the office came about in the New Testament church as a Spirit-led response to certain emerging needs and circumstances in a loose and fluid situation is most certainly unacceptable.

As we speak of elders we do well to remember that elders in the New Testament church were also called *bishops*, that is, *overseers*. That title carries meanings that don't mesh well with the notion of servanthood featured in report 44-1973.

Another omission in this significant document in the recent history of the Christian Reformed Church is the failure to reflect on the position of prominence accorded to elders in the book of Revelation. In John's vision of the heavenly scene there were twenty-four elders seated on twenty-four thrones surrounding the great throne occupied by the glorious one worshipped by the elders. Repeatedly the elders come into prominence in this grand book of Holy Scripture. Certainly it takes no special pleading to maintain that the position of the elders in Revelation is hardly adequately described by the particular concept of servanthood that dominates report 44-1973.

47

Report 44-1973 vs. the Belgic Confession

Synod 1972, in expressing its dissatisfaction with the report on Ecclesiastical Office and Ordination (Report Number 40 then), referred the report back to the study committee with a mandate which in part asked the committee "to delineate the comparison between its conclusions and Articles 30, 31 of the Belgic Confession" (*Acts of Synod 1972*, p. 95).

Report 44-1973 dealt with this mandate. (See *Acts of Synod 1973*, pp. 709-711). Article 32 of the Confession was also taken into account. One is hard pushed to accept as credible the claim of the authors of 44-1973 that "our report and its conclusions are basically in line with the Confession." I do not find in these Articles of the Belgic Confession the purely functional notion of the special offices, in which the New Testament church is looked upon as a loose fellowship developing new services (offices) as circumstances dictated. The authors of the report judged, according to their Guideline Number Twelve, that "the Bible leaves room for the church to adapt or modify its special ministries in order to carry out its service to Christ effectively in all circumstances."

The Confession, let it be noted well, speaks of "that spiritual polity which our Lord taught us in His Word; namely, that there must be ministers or pastors ... elders and deacons, who ... form the council of the Church." The Confession goes on to say that ministers of the Word "have equally the same power and authority wheresoever they are, as they are all ministers of Christ." And our church accepts this admonition, "Moreover, in order that this holy ordinance of God may not be violated or slighted, we say that every one ought to esteem the ministers of God's Word and the elders of the Church very highly for their work's sake ..."

Article 32 of the Confession states, "though it is useful and beneficial that those who are rulers of the Church institute and establish certain ordinances among themselves for maintaining the body of the Church, yet they ought studiously to take care that they do not depart from those things which Christ, our only Master, has instituted."

Do these citations from the Confession sound like they describe a church that can be spoken of as a fluid, loose affair in which new offices emerge as circumstances or need may indicate? To this writer it is eloquently evident that when the authors of 44-1973 claimed that "our report and its conclusions are basically in line with the Confession," they furnished us with one more expression of an opinion that has been voiced frequently in recent years. This opinion is the judgment that certain challenged teachings are within the bounds of the confessions of the church. In many instances (such as with respect to views set forth by Kuitert and Wiersenga in the Netherlands) this opinion has left one with the feeling that the bounds of the confessions must be made of very, very elastic rubber. This is my feeling with respect to the claim of the authors of report 44-1973.

What About The Laying On Of Hands?

The service in which an office-bearer in the church is ordained is usually an impressive affair. In the case of the ordination of a minister of the Word this is done with the reading of a prescribed form and the laying on of hands. So far in this chapter we have concentrated on the meaning of office in the church and have said nothing about ordination. Greater attention has to be given to the matter of office because one's understanding of the meaning of ordination is bound up with one's view of the special offices.

If one views office in the way in which 44-1973 views it, namely, as adequately described by the word *function* within a loose and fluid situation in which any service that may be regarded as being for the good of the church is an office, then one's idea of ordination can well be reduced to symbolizing *appointment,* as is the case in 44-1973.

What about this designation of office as function? Of course, each office is a function. But what has then been said? Very little. One has said very little when he describes a ratel to a questioner with the simple word "animal." Hundreds of other creatures are covered by that word, from mice to elephants. So too there are all sorts of functions performed in the church. Are they all to be regarded as special offices? That can happen only "under the guidance of the Spirit" according to Guideline Number Four.

Just how are we to understand this "guidance of the Spirit?" Under what circumstances does this guidance occur? Who is to determine when the Spirit leads the church to recognize some function as an office? There are important special ministries in the church like that of music director, Sunday School teacher, organist, "Coffee Break" leader, youth leader. Should some or all of these be members of the church council? It seems that there are instances in which those functioning in these special ministries are in actuality very much involved in the management of the church. Could this development be seen by some as evidence of the Spirit's guidance in making some function an office in the church? The establishment of such office could be viewed as a means of doing Christ's work in the world more "efficiently and effectively."

It is evident that we get into all sorts of problem areas when we follow the functional notion of office as that is developed in 44-1973. As a consequence our concept of ordination loses character, and "appointment" would seem to be an adequate description of this solemn event in the life of the church.

On the other hand, if the offices are what they are described as being in the church's Confession, then ordination will symbolize something more then mere appointment. As we have seen, according to the Confession the offices in the church constitute "that spiritual polity which our Lord has taught us in His Word." Those holding office have "power and authority," and they are "rulers of the church."

Scripture makes clear that the laying on of hands involves considerably more than mere appointment. When the high priest placed his hands on the head of the scapegoat he put the sins of the people on the goat's head (Lev. 16:21). Joshua, on becoming leader of Israel, "was filled with the spirit of wisdom because Moses had laid his hands on him" (Deut. 34:9). When Paul met some disciples at Ephesus who did not know about the Holy Spirit, he taught them and when he "laid his hands on them, the Holy Spirit came on them, and they spoke in tongues and prophesied" (Acts 19:6). When Peter and John placed their hands on certain Samaritans "they received the Holy Spirit" (Acts 8:17). Paul admonished Timothy, "Do not neglect your gift, which was given you through a prophetic message when the body of elders laid their hands on you" (I Tim. 4:14).

It would be presumptuous to try to make a definitive statement as to just exactly what is involved in the ceremony of ordination. Let it be suggested here that, with a higher conception of office in view than that set forth in Report 44-1973, ordination symbolizes the presence of whatever gifts the Holy Spirit has conferred on the ordinand together with bestowal of that special spiritual authority from the Head of the church that is needed so that the one being ordained may use his gifts effectively for the blessing of God's people.

44-1972 And 44-1973 Come Together

Just how much actual influence the Guidelines stemming from 44-1973 have had in the church is hard to assess. These Guidelines helped the Christian Reformed Church to come to the decision to establish the office of Evangelist as defined in the *Acts of Synod 1978*, pages 77-78. This decision came after more than thirty years of wrestling with the question of the official place of layworkers in evangelism in the work of the church. What further indentifiable impact this report has had is a question to which various answers would no doubt be given. The care with which different committees and succeeding synods dealt with the office of evangelist matter would seem to indicate that the freewheeling notion of church office presented in 44-1973 has not found general acceptance in the church.

However, the matter of serious concern is the manner in which Report 44-1973 handled the Bible. As we have sought to demonstrate earlier in this chapter, the interpretation of certain relevant passages of Scripture was bent to conform to a preconceived notion of the special ministries in the church. In other words, the teaching of the Bible as authoritative truth was determined by the particular bent of mind of the interpreters rather than by a careful, submissive, objective study done according to the accepted canons of Reformed biblical exegesis. In short, the way in which exegesis was done in 44-1973 looks very much like an example of the tendency we detected in Report 44-1972 on Biblical Authority, in which the authority or truth quality of the Bible was seen as dependent on man's understanding of the message of the Bible. In both reports the truth character of the Bible is in actuality viewed as relative to the mindset of the reader of Scripture.

The Bible is the truth and has authority just because it is the Word of God and not because of the way man thinks about the Bible. Parts of Report 44-1972 departed from this basic position, and in practice Report 44-1973 departed from it too. In this fundamental sense both documents have contributed to the decay of theological discussion in the church, and have therefore contributed to a slippage in confessional integrity, particularly with respect to the matter of the real authority of our only sure rule of faith and life – God's written Word.

CHAPTER 6
Does the Christian Reformed Church Have A Church Order?

Does the Christian Reformed Church have a Church Order? The obvious answer would seem to be that the church does in fact have a Church Order. Any one can just ask for a copy at the denominational headquarters in Grand Rapids and he will quickly have a booklet in his hands with the words CHURCH ORDER printed on the cover.

Still the question has to be asked: does the Christian Reformed Church have a Church Order? That question breaks down into two further questions. The first is this: is that which is called the Church Order in the Christian Reformed Church a manual of church usages and practices, or is it a true constitutional document by which the church "regulates its ecclesiastical organization and activities" (from Article I of the Church Order)?

The second question that we have to ask is this: what is the place of the Church Order in the Christian Reformed Church in actual practice? How steadfastly and consistently does the church observe proper procedure according to the articles of the Church Order in "complete subjection to the Word of God and the Reformed creeds" (from Article I)?

Let it be said at this early stage of our discussion that the history of the Christian Reformed Church reveals a body of believers with a high view of the Church Order, in theory and in practice. I have always seen the Christian Reformed Church in this light.

There probably are a number of reasons for this history of high regard for good order in the church. One of these reasons is surely found in Article 29 of the Church Order itself. Here we read as follows, "Decisions of ecclesiastical assemblies shall be reached upon due consideration. The decisions of the assemblies shall be considered settled and binding unless it

53

is proved that they conflict with the Word of God or the Church Order." The very next article deals with the right of appeal. An article similar to the one just quoted appeared as Article 31 in the Church Order prior to the extensive revision of 1965.

The highly significant point in this citation from the Church Order is that in the estimation of the church the Church Order is put on a virtual par with the Bible so far as the government of the church is concerned. We are not arguing here, of course, that the two are equal. But it is obvious from such wording that the Church Order is meant to be decisively important in the Christian Reformed Church. It may not be taken lightly. People may not play games with it. In all the procedures and deliverances in the church the Word of God must rule, and, under that rule, the church "regulates its ecclesiastical organization and activities" by the articles of the Church Order. That which is contrary to the Church Order has no place in the church.

"Shall Be Faithfully Observed"

However, it does appear that not all members of the Christian Reformed Church hold this high view of the Church Order. An editorial in *The Banner* of October 29, 1984 dealt with the results of a study done by the Social Research Center at Calvin College. One finding of the study was that a majority of the readers believed that the editor of the magazine should always defend the Reformed confessions. Another finding indicated that a majority of the readers felt the editor "should not always defend Christian Reformed practices and traditions." The words "practices and traditions" came, it would seem, from the group doing the study and were not the editor's language. Nothing is said in the article about the Church Order. Did the group doing the study place the Church Order under "Christian Reformed practices and traditions?" Did those readers who shared the majority opinion understand the words "practices and traditions" to refer to the Church Order? Would they have answered as they did if the survey had asked whether they thought the editor should always defend the Church Order? Such questions arise regarding the article in *The Banner*. What is clear is that the Church Order did not fare very well in the project. One has to assume it was not thought to be worth mentioning, or that it was placed under "Christian Reformed practices and traditions."

Such downgrading of the Church Order does not mesh well with what Article 29 has to say, as we have seen. Nor does such downgrading mesh well with the declaration in the final article of the Church Order, where it is flatly stated that the Church Order "shall be faithfully observed" (Article 96). An older respected commentator has expressed well what has historically been the reigning attitude toward the Church Order when he wrote that these "ecclesiastical stipulations bear a regulatory character and bind the conscience only insofar as they are drawn from Scripture. The Church Order has a binding character in church affairs and places the members and officebearers under obligation to maintain it."[1]

Frequent Changes

If the requirements of the Church Order are to be observed in church government and administration in much the same way that the teaching of Scripture is to be honored and if these stipulations are to be faithfully observed, it follows that the text of the Church Order should be reasonably constant. Frequent changes do not comport with the faithful observance that is called for.

Frequent changes? Almost every year since 1965, the year of a major overhaul of the Church Order, there have been changes. As recently as 1987 many changes were proposed and these were adopted with minor editorial alterations and additions in 1988. The many changes proposed in 1987 prompted the officers of the Synod to take the unusual step of making a recommendation. The recommendation, which was adopted, reads as follows:

That synod appoint a committee to study the Church Order, its Supplements, and other synodical rules and regulations, which pertain to the Church Order, and make recommendations about their organization and codification to the Synod of 1989.

---

[1]Joh. Jansen, *Korte Verklaring Van De Kerkenordening*, Kampen, J. H. Kok, 1923, p. 2.

Grounds

A. The Church Order itself is intended to be a clear and stable statement of church government. Frequent changes and substantial additions of recent years undermine its stability and its authority.

B. Several changes and additions to the Church Order made recently may well be more appropriately placed in the synodical regulations.

C. Synod needs a criterion for determining when a decision affecting church government is a change in the Church Order requiring ratification by a succeeding synod (*1987 Acts of Synod*, pp. 651-652).

Ground A of this significant recommendation deserves careful note. The officers did not regard the Church Order as being a mere manual of practices and usages in the Christian Reformed Church. They thought of it as a document "intended to be a clear and stable statement of church government." In other words, they thought of it as a church constitution. As such, it should not be altered too freely, lest its stability and authority be undermined.

"Synodical Regulations"

The extensive revision of the Church Order in 1965 carried within itself the threat of diminishing stature. Does this document have the character of a basic constitution? This question was raised regarding the proposed revised Church Order. A future professor at Calvin Seminary raised the question in this way, "In general, I believe that the entire proposed revision is far too lengthy and detailed. There is much material in this revision which could well be omitted, and which is hardly constitutional material. A good constitution . . . should say as much as possible in as few words as possible, and should establish the basic principles which shall govern and guide the church."[2]

The present writer expressed his concern from a different perspective. He was troubled by the frequency (fifteen times) of the words "synodical regulations" in the proposed revision, as, for example, in the proposed Article 55c (later Article 52c), "The consistory shall see to it that choirs, and others who sing

---

[2]R. R. De Ridder, writing in *Torch and Trumpet*, March 1963, p. 14.

in the worship services, observe the synodical regulations governing the content of the hymns and anthems sung." The question was asked, "Does such language used again and again suggest that this document is a primary document, a *constitution* of the church? Or do such repeated references suggest that this document is somehow subordinate to a body of synodical regulations that constitute the actual rule of the church in all these affairs? The impression left on the writer is plainly the latter."[3]

It should be noted that the Church Order prior to the revision of 1965 contained no such language. There were only four references to *regulations* or *ordinances* that had to be observed, but they were called "ecclesiastical" or "general ecclesiastical" ordinances or regulations. The adjective *synodical* was not used. The difference was indeed striking, and in the mind of the present writer the older Church Order reflected a much finer sensitivity to basic principles of Reformed church polity. The Church Order currently in use in the Christian Reformed Church still contains fifteen such references.

The frequent use of the words "synodical regulations" cannot fail to suggest and promote a tendency toward "rule from the top" in the church. And that means increasing rule by a church bureaucracy. It is not surprising, therefore, that with growing frequency we today are hearing complaints about just such a drift in the church. Such complaints commonly carry expressions like synodocracy, growing bureaucracy, bureaucratic arrogance, church strong at the top, and even the words synodical tyranny.

Amending The Constitution
The officers of Synod 1987 said, "The Church Order is intended to be a clear and stable statement of church government. Frequent changes and substantial additions of recent years undermine its stability and authority."

This clear and straightforward statement by these leaders in the church deserves thoughtful consideration. The concern of these men has been a burden to others. Overtures asking that a vote calling for more than a simple majority at synod be required in matters involving changes in the Confessions

---

[3]E. Heerema, writing in *Torch and Trumpet*, March 1963, p. 10.

and Church Order appeared at the Synods of 1976, 1977, and especially 1979. In 1979 six such overtures appeared, all but one from Classes. The 1976 overture argued as follows, "To add to or change our constitution, which we believe to be based on the Word of God and which we as officebearers are bound to uphold by the Form of Subscription, on the basis of a fifty percent plus one vote majority is against all common sense. One would be hard pressed to find another association or body where the constitution could be changed in this fashion" (*Acts of Synod 1976*, p. 628). In 1979 Classis Huron argued as follows for its overture calling for a majority vote of two-thirds of the delegates at synod on a proposed change in the Church Order, "This will prevent a small majority from forcing its will upon the total life of the denomination" (*Acts of Synod 1979*, p. 682). Other good grounds were given for these requests that the method of changing the church's constitution be improved.

This subject drew the attention of a former close student of church polity and he had this to say, "Revision of our Church Order is comparatively easy – and this involves a great risk. Majorities in Synods shift easily and rapidly. Our Church should safeguard itself against the present ease of revision by requiring approval of a proposed amendment by some rule similar to those of other denominations."[4] The author, J. L. Shaver, referred to the rule in the Reformed Church in America which called for approval of a proposed amendment by two-thirds of the Classes, and to the rule in the Presbyterian churches that required approval by a majority of the Presbyteries before an amendment could go into effect. The rationale for a proposed change in the church's basic law ought to be so clear and persuasive that such change should be acceptable to a large majority of the delegates to synod or of the Classes or consistories. Under the present arrangement a concerted effort to win a bare majority of the votes at a synod can make important changes in the church's constitution. This is not as it should be. The conference of apostles and elders at Jerusalem described in Acts 15 (sometimes called the first synod or general assembly), came,

---

[4]J. L. Shaver, *The Polity of the Churches*, Vol II. 4th Ed. Rev., 1956, p. 60.

it seems, to a unanimous decision on some critical questions affecting the expanding church. (See especially Acts 15:22 and 25). Making critical decisions affecting the teaching and government of the church by a bare majority vote hardly does justice to the pattern we find in Acts 15. It is hard to believe that a synod can adopt a change in its constitution with the words "it seemed good to the Holy Spirit and to us" when almost half of the Spirit-led church is opposed to the change.

"Faithfully Observed"

We are asking the question, "Does the Christian Reformed Church have a Church Order?" Under that general question it is altogether proper that one ask whether the provisions of the Church Order are "faithfully observed" in the church.

Earlier it has been stated here that the history of the Christian Reformed Church has been marked by a high level of faithful observance of the provisions of the Church Order. But for some time now troublesome doubts on this score have been pressing upon us. For instance, with altogether too much frequency reports are heard of violations of Article 54b of the Church Order. This article stipulates, "At one of the services each Lord's Day, the minister shall ordinarily preach the Word as summarized in the Heidelberg Catechism, following its sequence." Furthermore, statements are made with disturbing frequency that many congregations do pretty much as they please, regardless of the requirements of the Church Order. And then there are those who are saying that the denomination seems to be drifting toward congregationalism instead of following a consistently Reformed church polity.

For the purposes of this chapter the writer feels it will be most helpful to deal with specific violations of an instrument that holds a very special place in the government of the Christian Reformed Church. Article 89a of the Church Order states, "Special discipline shall be applied to officebearers if they violate the Form of Subscription." What are the main elements in this document that every minister, elder, deacon, evangelist and professor (at Calvin College and Seminary) signs? First of all the signatories "declare truthfully and in good conscience before the Lord that we sincerely believe that all the articles and points of doctrine set forth" in the confessions of the church "fully agree with the Word of God," and they "promise therefore to teach these doctrines diligently, to defend them faithfully, and not to contradict them, publicly or privately, directly or indirectly, in our preaching, teaching, or writing."

Secondly, the signatories "promise further that if in the future we come to have any difficulty with these doctrines or reach views differing from them, we will not propose, defend, preach, or teach such views, either publicly or privately, until we have first disclosed them to the consistory, classis, or synod for examination."

In the third place the signatories pledge that "if, to maintain unity and purity in doctrine, the consistory, classis, or synod considers it proper at any time – on sufficient grounds of concern – to require a fuller explanation of our views concerning any article" in the church's three confessions, "we are always willing and ready to comply with such a request." These quotations are from the new rendering of the text of the Form of Subscription adopted in 1988.

The language of the Form of Subscription is plain. The requirements of the Church Order are clear. Have these plain terms so solemnly agreed to, been honored in the church? In the main, yes. However, when one examines the public writings of one who has held a very important and sensitive position in the church, namely, that of editor of *The Banner* from 1980 to 1989, we have to ask in all seriousness just what faithful compliance with the terms of the Church Order and the Form of Subscription meant to the editor and to the church.

Views of the Editor

In 1981 (*The Banner* issues of Oct. 26 and Dec. 7) the editor declared, "The views of the Reformers are no longer ours. And the kind of thinking that is recorded in the Belgic Confession is no longer functional in the Christian Reformed Church." The author of these words has solemnly averred before the church of Christ that he is "persuaded that all the articles and points of doctrine contained in the Confession . . . do fully agree with the Word of God." Thus in 1981 the editor wrote that certain teachings of the Word of God are no longer meaningful or usable in the Christian Reformed Church. He was referring to Articles 27, 28 and 29 of the Confession of Faith.

In dealing with the question of children at the Lord's Supper in *The Banner* of March 26, 1984, the editor proposed that "we disconnect admission to the Lord's Supper and public profession of faith." This proposal goes directly contrary to Article 59a of the Church Order.

The issues of September 23 and October 14 of 1985 carried editorials on Jacob Arminius, the theologian whose views were repudiated in the Canons of Dort. Speaking in a laudatory fashion of this theologian, the editor made clear that his new understanding of the seventh chapter of Romans, an understanding also taught by Arminius, disagrees with Question-Answer 114 of the Heidelberg Catechism. He might have added that his new view also disagrees with Question-Answers 60 and 62 of the Catechism. Placing the Synod of Dort and its work in an unfavorable light, the editor also quoted a judgment that says, "If there are still people to be found who think Arminius got a square deal at the hands of the 'orthodoxy' of his time, these too must read" a certain book referred to. We remember that the editor signed the Form in which he pledged to "reject all errors . . . and particularly those which were condemned by the above mentioned Synod." Although the special reference to the work of the Synod of Dort has been dropped at this point in the new contemporary rendering of the Form of Subscription adopted in 1988, the pledge to "reject all errors that conflict" with the creeds of the church is still binding.

In 1985 the editor said in the issue of October 28, "Even in our church the confessions are losing their hold. The three forms of unity fail to give us a common frame of reference for understanding both the Bible and our mission in the world." To relieve the growing irrelevance of the creeds as he saw it the editor would have ministers and professors quit talking about "renewed study of the confessions and a better translation of the creeds." Instead he would have them "admit difficulties in the confessions themselves."

The above examples portray a pattern of editorializing in the church's official magazine that surely does not demonstrate loyalty to the Form of Subscription that the editor has signed. Many voices have been raised against such writing and also against the editor's selection of writers and materials for publication. One such troubled voice had this to say, "How refreshing it would be to read even one issue of *The Banner* in which our Reformed creeds, historic forms, and moral heritage were supported instead of attacked and derided" (issue of October

10, 1983). We recall that the editor had pledged to teach and faithfully defend the teaching of the church's confessions "without either *directly* or *indirectly* contradicting the same by our public preaching or *writing*" (italics by EH).

How did the editor feel about the Form of Subscription? We have a clue in the above examples from his writings. In *The Banner* of June 27, 1983 he wrote more directly as follows, "The Form of Subscription has become an ecclesiastical yoke by which orthodoxy is to be maintained; and we aren't so sure it is the yoke of Christ. The form functions as a device to keep the lid on. It has paralyzed the teachers of the church . . ." This scornful evaluation appeared in an editorial which expressed sympathy with Harry Boer's screaming (the editor's word) reaction to the failure of the synod to deal favorably with his gravamen against the Canons of Dort in the teaching of reprobation.

In the issue of February 13, 1989 the editor had more to say about the Form of Subscription. Here his critical view of the Form concentrates once again on the place of the Canons of Dort in the document he has signed. His opinion is that "the canons and the rejections ratified in 1618 and 1619 are too complicated for most of our church members, including the majority of officebearers, to understand." The editor wants a Form that addresses current aberrations such as those propagated by Mormons and Muslims. "We must not pretend," argued the editor, "that the fight is still against the Remonstrants," and "We must not, with our Form of Subscription, try to live in a little world of our own." Such comments reflect a warped view of the matter. Love for and devotion to the Canons of Dort are not incompatible with a passion for contemporaneity. No one fully alive to the blessed and changeless relevance of the gospel would wish to argue against the desirability of a testimony that answers clearly the distorted claims of the false prophets of our day. But the church's Reformed witness is not helped by such oblique attacks on a creed that has given christendom its finest statement of the meaning of the central glorious teaching of Christianity, namely, salvation by grace in the redeeming work of the triune God.

Incidentally it is to the point to remind ourselves that the Christian Reformed Church, by action of synod in 1976, not only refused to replace or revise the Form of Subscription, but also laid down guidelines to be followed in making known to the church "any difficulties or different sentiments" an officebearer may have regarding the confessions of the church. The communication by which such "difficulty with these doctrines . . . or views differing from them" (1988 rendering of the Form) are made known to the church is called a "gravamen."

It is fully apparent from the examples taken from the editor's writings that he has difficulties with the confessions of the church. Has he brought these difficulties to his supervising consistory by means of a gravamen? It seems abundantly clear that he should have done this in more than one instance.

An Overture Regarding The Editor's Views

An overture addressed to Synod 1985 requested the church to examine the views of the editor at an important point. The account of what the church did with that overture reads like a kind of Alice in Wonderland adventure in ecclesiastical procedure. A brief account of this strange affair is presented here as a not so reassuring example of how the church sometimes deals with issues that confront it.

In *The Banner* of January 23, 1984 the editor wrote, that "the restricted role of women in the service of worship" prescribed by the Apostle Paul in I Corinthians 14:34 and I Timothy 2:12 was determined by reasons that were "local, cultural, and therefore temporal." Classis Florida adopted without dissenting vote an overture to be forwarded to synod in which the exegesis of the editor was questioned. The term "local," for example, is not valid for Paul plainly says that the rule holds "in all the congregations of the saints" (I Cor. 14:33). The Classis requested that the editor be asked to give "further explanation" of his understanding of the Articles V and VII of the Confession of Faith. In Article V the church confesses that the books of the Bible are for the "regulation, foundation, and confirmation of our faith; believing without any doubt all things contained in them . . ." In Article VII we confess that the "doctrine" of the Word of God is "most perfect and complete in all respects." Also, Article VII says that we may not consider "custom . . . or succession of times and persons . . . of equal value with the truth of God." This part of the Confession was contradicted by the editor's claim that Paul's teaching was bound to outworn customs and practices, so that changing times set aside the truth of God, thus making "custom . . . or succession of times and persons . . . of equal value with the truth of God."[5]

What prompted Classis Florida to pass the overture without dissenting voice? Animosity toward the editor? Not at all. The overriding concern was the seriousness of the matter. "The issues raised in this overture," declared the Classis, "are of great significance and should be faced by the church. These issues are disturbing to many in the church and are raising troublesome questions for them with respect to the Holy Scriptures. What is to be understood by the cultural and temporal conditioning of the Bible? What does this mean in specific instances, like those raised by Rev. Kuyvenhoven? Does the acknowledgement of cultural and temporal conditioning mean that the Bible is a 'time-bound' book, as Kuitert and others have alleged? How does Kuyvenhoven's teaching differ from that of the old liberalism, which said flatly that the Bible is out of date? These and similar questions must be dealt with for the sake of the peace and witness of our beloved church."

A Strange Story

It soon became apparent after the overture had been sent in that it was running into trouble. I shall here relate as succinctly as I can some strange twists and turns of the path this legally passed overture with its deep concern took through ecclesiastical channels.

The trouble began with the one to whom the overture was properly sent, the Stated Clerk of the denomination. Word came that he had problems with the overture. I wrote him about this prior to the meeting of Classis Florida at which the overture was adopted. In his answer, dated December 27, 1984, he wrote as follows, "The Form of Subscription refers to a person revealing his views to the 'consistory, classis or synod,' and readiness to submit to the judgment of the 'consistory, classis, or synod.' I do not interpret this to suggest that persons may go directly to classis or synod and thereby avoid the regular procedural steps of appeal." The letter made no reference whatsoever to that section of the Form under which the classis made its request.

---

[5]For the full text of this overture see Appendix A.

The Stated Clerk drew the overture to the attention of the Church Polity and Program Committee, a sub-committee of the Synodical Interim Committee. Believing the overture was out of order, the committee decided it should not be printed in the Agenda for Synod. Prior to the meeting of synod the full Synodical Interim Committee decided to leave the question of the overture's place on the agenda to the officers of the Synod. The officers decided the overture was legally before synod, and synod acted on it.

It should be carefully noted at this point that a unit of the church's bureaucracy interfered with the movement of an overture from a classis to synod. The overture came from a proper, legal body in the church's government (a classis), and should have gone to the broader assembly to which it was sent, for that body to determine the overture's propriety and validity. Granted the members of the Church Polity and Program Committee acted in sincerity and without malice, but their action was nonetheless highhanded and cannot go unchallenged.

Synod 1985 rejected the overture on the following grounds, here abbreviated: (1) Classis Florida should have addresssed its request to the calling church, according to Article 13 of the Church Order; (b) the provisions of the Church Order do not set up a method of inquiry or discipline independent of that set forth in Articles 89, 90, 91, and 93 of the Church Order; and (c) rejection of the overture is in harmony with a precedent set by Synod 1976.

These grounds are hardly convincing. We comment on each as follows: (a) the second sentence of Article 13a allows for the kind of request made by Classis Florida; (b) it is not at all clear that the overture asked for a method of inquiry or discipline independent of that given in the cited articles of the Church Order; and (c) the precedent of 1976 is irrelevant, since the 1976 action related to an appeal regarding a candidate's classical examination, and so the candidate's ordination in the meantime called for a different approach directed to the newly ordained minister's calling church.

After the synod adopted the recommendation with its grounds, the body passed a motion declaring the overture out of order. This is indeed a curious twist in procedure, to declare a matter out of order after it has been acted on.

A Consistory Picks Up The Issue

The issue raised in the Florida overture did not die with the action of synod. The consistory of the First Christian Reformed Church of Orange City, Iowa, felt the issue was so serious that it should not be dropped. So the consistory did what synod's decision seemed to say they should do, namely, appeal to the consistory of the editor's calling church. The response of the supervising consistory was that they did not find sufficient grounds to warrant asking the editor for further explanation.

Appeal to Classis Grand Rapids East was next. This body declared the appeal out of order on a ground essentially the same as one of the grounds for the rejection of the Florida overture by Synod 1985, namely, that the "Form of Subscription does not provide a method of inquiry independent of or preliminary to Church Order Articles 89-93."

The issue came back to synod in 1988, by way of appeal from the decision of Classis Grand Rapids East. The story of the handling of this matter at Synod 1988 makes interesting reading, even puzzling reading at times. Apparently synod's Advisory Committee did not find the appeal a simple matter for them to handle. The report of this committee was not acceptable to synod and the matter was recommitted. The unsatisfactory report recommended that synod not sustain the appeal on the ground that "There are no formal charges or substantiated suspicions to support a formal inquiry" (*Acts of Synod 1988*, p. 545). It should be noted that the appeal was not declared out of order, as was done by Synod 1985 with the Florida overture after it had acted on the matter by adopting the recommendations of its Advisory Committee. Classis Grand Rapids East had also declared it out of order, on a ground taken over from the grounds adopted by Synod 1985. The confusion brought about by Synod 1985 in declaring the Florida overture out of order after it had been acted on appears anew in the 1988 Advisory Committee's report when it says that "the grounding of the classical decision in the *Acts of Synod 1985* is unfortunate because that statement was never acted upon by synod." Was it *never* acted on by Synod 1985?

The 1988 Advisory Committee came back with a report very different from that which was recommitted. The recommendation was much the same, but the grounds for it were very different. The *Analysis* was also very different. The *Analysis* and the grounds for the recommendation adopted by synod all zeroed in on a technicality involving some unfortunate language in the original request of First Orange City to the editor's supervising consistory. The request was made in language that assumed the consistory of First Orange City rather than the supervising consistory should ask the editor for a further explanation of his views. "We address this request to him through you his supervising consistory . . ." said the letter dated August 6, 1986. A church searching for grounds on which to dispose of this troublesome matter found this technical slipup most helpful. So the grounds for not sustaining this appeal with its weighty concern became these: (a) "The Church Order makes an officebearer formally accountable only to the consistory under which he serves"; (b) ". . . No officebearer pledges himself to give an account of his views to a neighboring consistory"; and (3) "A neighboring consistory does not have the right to request an officebearer's own consistory to act as its proxy" (*Acts of Synod 1988*, p. 613).

Questions About Synod's Performance

On first reading these grounds sound impressive. With further thought they leave one troubled. Does the church of Jesus Christ deal with an earnest concern of some of its members by throwing it out on a technicality of the kind we have here? The intent of the Orange City appeal was unmistakable. Neither the supervising consistory nor Classis Grand Rapids East dealt with the appeal by dismissing it on this technical ground. And synod should not have done so either. Rather than make the whole serious issue turn on such a technicality, the synod could have noted the error in a sentence, and then dealt with the real burden of the appeal by addressing the question of the sufficiency of the grounds of concern. Synod's action on the Orange City appeal made an honorable body look petty.

And there are other questions. In its *Analysis* synod's Advisory Committee said, "In the case of those serving the whole denomination under the jurisdiction of its synodical boards, one who signs the Form of Subscription pledges his readiness to give an account of his views to synod or its representative, the board of jurisdiction" (*Acts of Synod 1988*,, p. 612). These words jumped at me when I first read them. This was exactly what prompted Classis Florida to come directly to synod in

1985, as the editor was serving the whole denomination. But the Synod said the request should have been addressed to the supervising consistory.

An important question arises at this point. Does one signing the Form of Subscription "pledge his readiness to give an account of his views to synod *or its representative, the board of jurisdiction?*" (italics by EH). The words in italics were a gratuitous addition by the Advisory Committee. The signatory pledges his readiness to give "further explanation" of his views only to a proper ecclesiastical judicatory (consistory, classis or synod). Only such may properly make judgments regarding an officebearer's loyalty to the faith the church confesses. A board can only make judgments as to a person's competence to serve in a particular position and to articulate the faith well in accordance with the character and demands of the position he holds under the board's jurisdiction.[6]

What is of immediate interest is the fact that the words quoted above from the *Analysis* of the Advisory committee contradict the first ground of synod's decision. Here we read, "The Church Order makes an officebearer formally accountable only to the consistory under which he serves."

But, someone may object, synod did not adopt the *Analysis* of the Advisory Committee; it adopted only its recommendation with the grounds. The point is correct. However, the contradiction also appears in a paragraph containing advice adopted by synod on the proper procedure to follow in such cases. The advice reads as follows:

> When a *consistory* judges that it has sufficient grounds of suspicion against an officebearer not under its supervision, it may communicate such to that officebearer's consistory or synodical

---

[6]The writer is quite aware of the fact that the history of the Christian Reformed Church does not unambiguously support his argumentation at this point. This is an important issue which the church should address. The problem arises also in the examination of candidates for ordination by the Board of Trustees of Calvin College and Seminary, a representative of synod. This important ecclesiastical function should be performed by a proper ecclesiastical body, not by a representative of such.

board under which the officebearer serves. If the officebearer's consistory and/or synodical board then judges that the grounds of suspicion are insufficient to require further explanation, the procedure ends. If the suspicions are judged to be sufficient, the consistory must follow the regulations of the Church Order and the denominational board must refer the matter to the synod.

The contradiction referred to above is obvious. In fact, this paragraph of advice indicates that there are instances in which the supervising consistory can be by-passed completely. This is wholly at variance with the debatable contention that was voiced at almost every point in the processing of this overture/appeal, namely, that the body seeking further explanation must always deal with the supervising consistory. We bear in mind that the advice quoted above has to do with an officebearer not under the supervision of the consistory seeking further explanation.

Another point worth observing in the advice is the statement that the "procedure ends" when the supervising consistory or the synodical board does not find the grounds of suspicion sufficient. Is this now part of the Church Order? Is this now one of the Synodical Regulations that the Church Order speaks of so often? What about the complainant's right of appeal under the terms of Church Order Article 30a? Are rulings such as this one, adopted by a synod without due process of overture, study and proper approval, to be considered binding on the church? Can future assemblies appeal to this language as ground for action, as Classis Grand Rapids East did in its use of the ground taken from the curious action of Synod 1985?

With this flawed performance by Synod 1988 the Florida overture/Orange City appeal ended its journey through the ecclesiastical channels of the Christian Reformed Church. It was a rough journey, marked by ambiguities, contradictions and many questions. This rocky road could have been avoided if Synod had dealt with the classical overture in an orderly fashion as laid out in the Form of Subscription, Article 13a of the Church Order, and ample precedent in similar cases in the history of the Christian Reformed Church. At the end of this long path one has to ask whether the church did not itself violate the terms of the Church Order and the Form of Subscription.

In Conclusion

This chapter has become longer than the author wanted it to be. The subject has its intricacies. But it is hoped that the discussion enhances the pertinence of the question, "Does the Christian Reformed Church have a Church Order?"

Many questions have surfaced in our study of this matter. Most of these questions need not be repeated. But we must ask again, does the church have a true constitution, or is that which is called the Church Order actually only a handbook of usages and practices? Does the relative ease and the frequency with which the Church Order has been changed in recent years enhance the church's regard for its form of government?

Certain notions and practices that have developed raise serious questions as to the standing of the Church Order and the Form of Subscription in the church. This chapter has looked carefully at the manner in which a sincere concern about an officebearer's views was handled. Precedents set in 1918, 1922, 1936, 1959, 1961 and 1963 simply do not support the contention that such concerns must always be addressed to the supervising consistory. The precedents of 1961 and 1963 are especially pertinent and illuminating. In 1961 a consistory went directly to synod requesting that a pastor be asked to give further explanation of his views as these had been expressed in a magazine article. Synod declared that the overture was legally before synod on the ground that "the Form of Subscription gives this consistory the right to bring this matter directly to Synod" (*Acts of Synod 1961,* p. 100). In 1963 a classis, without first going to the officebearer involved or his consistory, came directly to synod with an overture requesting that a professor be asked to give further explanation of his views as these had been expressed in some published writings. Synod took the overture to be in order and acted on it, deciding not to accede on the ground that the classis "did not submit sufficient grounds for its suspicion" (*Acts of Synod 1963,* p. 95).

The special discipline called for in Articles 89-93 of the Church Order is first of all the responsibility of the supervising consistory. But whether in a particular instance such special discipline should be applied is a question that usually requires the judgment of the broader fellowship of the church. Is it reasonable or realistic to expect a consistory to question or to take action against a brother whom they have called, one who is part of the congregation's loving fellowship, one with whom the consistory has labored? Such questioning or action is likely only when the person involved has proved himself to be obnoxious or outspokenly heretical. In 1918, for example, a consistory refused to accept synod's judgment against their pastor's views and thus refused to initiate discipline against him, leaving it to the classis to exercise the discipline called for.

It is twenty-five years since the Christian Reformed Church adopted a major revision of its Church Order. That is a short time compared to the longevity of the text of the Church Order prior to 1965. Yet, the time may have come for another careful evaluation of the Church Order. The many questions that have emerged in this study and the confusion and fumbling that marked the handling of the legitimate concern brought by a classis and then a consistory would seem to underline the need for such a fresh look. From our study it seems apparent that the church has in actual practice lost a tool that has proved to be very useful in maintaining the church as a fellowship true to its Biblical faith and its confessional moorings. I refer to that section of the Form of Subscription in which the signatory declares himself "always ready and willing" to give "a fuller explanation" of his views to consistory, classis, or synod on "sufficient grounds of concern." Does the church really want to give up this useful and previously effective tool?

One reason for the request for a new study of the Church Order which the officers of Synod 1987 made was that "Several changes and additions to the Church Order made recently may well be more appropriately placed in the synodical regulations." The church needs a stable constitution that contains in clear, succinct language the important ruling articles of church government, together with the body of by-laws or ecclesiastical regulations that have been adopted in the application of these guiding principles to the ongoing life and government of this precious part of the body of Christ.

71

CHAPTER 7
Creation or Evolution

For a large part of its history the Christian Reformed Church has kept a wary eye open for the possible appearance of the teaching of evolution. Behind this wariness was the conviction that the teaching of creation is fundamental in the Christian faith. This is the foundation on which all else in the faith is built. Creation anchors the Christian-theistic view of life and history. Correlative with this basic conviction is the belief that evolutionary thinking and the Biblical teaching of creation are flat incompatible.

In more recent times the watchfulness with regard to evolutionary teaching has undergone a change. The enemy has taken on a different, more attractive face. When evolution was presented as a purely naturalistic development by which life was explained, rejection of the teaching was the fairly obvious Christian thing to do. But then came *theistic* evolution.

When this effort to blend the Biblical teaching of creation with evolution first appeared is a question that need not occupy us now. For our purposes it is enough to point out that concern about the appearance of this brand of evolutionism in the Christian Reformed Church flared up in the sixties. Three overtures brought this matter to synod in 1966. These overtures referred to various articles that had appeared on the subject and to confusion among the church membership about these teachings and their compatibility with the Bible. One overture alleged that "there are a number of our ministers, teachers, professional people and laymen, who profess to accept these teachings as scriptural" (*Acts of Synod 1966,* p. 550). Another overture, brought in 1967, claimed that it was becoming "increasingly obvious . . . that theistic evolution is being taught as an acceptable explanation of origins in our Church college" (*Acts of Synod 1967,* p. 717).

Nothing came of this flurry of excitement over the subject in the sixties. Synod 1966 appointed a committee of six to advise the next synod with respect to the proper manning of a commission to study the subject and the specific mandate under which such a commission should work. The committee came to Synod 1967 with the names of eight men to make up the proposed commission together with a broad, demanding mandate that called for specific attention to "the nature of the Divine revelation in Gen. 1-11," and "the essential teaching of Gen. 1-11 regarding the origin of the universe and of man" (*Acts of Synod 1967*, pp. 337-338). The Synod backed away from the extensive project with its delicate issues and decided to "withhold action." The reason given for this decision was that no specific case was before it challenging the "Scriptural and creedal teaching of creation by divine fiat," and thus the study called for was "not necessary at this time."

A Book Stirs The Church

All of this changed in 1986. Then Dr. Howard J. Van Till, professor of Physics and Astronomy at Calvin College, came out with a book entitled *The Fourth Day*. The book is a forthright exposition of an evolutionary understanding of the universe and all that is in it. So the book holds to the position of theistic evolution, although the author prefers to call it by another name – "creationomic science." He has chosen this term because it "emphasizes that God governs his Creation in a lawful manner." The suffix *nomic* comes from the Greek word for law – *nomos*. (See *The Fourth Day*, p. 213, footnote).

A virtual firestorm of criticism and protest was sparked by the publication of this book. Many critical articles have appeared in various places. The Board of Trustees of Calvin College and Seminary dealt with the matter by appointing an *ad hoc* committee to evaluate Van Till's writing as well as the published views of two of his colleagues, Dr. Clarence Menninga and Dr. Davis Young. The committee's mild criticism of these views was adopted by the Board of Trustees. Many in the church were not satisfied with this handling of the issue. The Board brought the matter to Synod 1988, and thirty-two overtures on the issue also came before the body. In the main the Synod followed the line of the Board. Adding to the intensity of feeling over the issue was the fact that an alumnus of the college whose several children also attended the school spent thousands of dollars to purchase a number of full-page ads in the Grand

Rapids daily newspaper to give vent to his frustration and distress at what was being taught at his alma mater.

We pause to take note of the difference between the way this problem at Calvin College was handled and the way a similar problem was dealt with at Dordt College in northwest Iowa. A professor of Dordt made statements at a conference held in 1987 which seemed to suggest sympathy for the theory of evolution. The Board of Trustees of the college appointed a committee to investigate. About a year later the committee reported that the professor had made clear to them that he rejected both evolution and theistic evolution. At the same time it was reported that a classroom syllabus used by the professor contained statements that seemed to contradict his avowed position. As a result, for the time being and while divisional discussions continued, the professor did not teach an introductory course in geology, and the syllabus referred to was withdrawn.

The Synod took no action with respect to the continued teaching of theistic evolution at Calvin College. A committee of ten members was appointed to study for three years the issues involved in the dispute over the evolutionary views of the professors. So the difference in the handling of these issues at the two schools is striking, especially so as we observe the fact that Calvin College is owned and operated by the Christian Reformed Church and Dordt College is owned and operated by a society of Reformed believers.

Perhaps the publication of this book by Professor Van Till can be seen as a salutary development. Now the church has opportunity to see for itself and to evaluate some crucially important teaching at Calvin College. We have observed that two decades earlier there were those who were troubled about the teaching of evolution at the college, but the church saw no proper opening for examining the matter at that time. With the appearance of *The Fourth Day* the issue with its many interrelated questions must now be squarely faced. Here is a thoughtful book that seeks to take the Bible and science seriously in the effort to resolve a conflict that has troubled many Christians over many years, the conflict between the theory of evolution and the teaching of the Bible on the question of origins and related matters.

Is Theistic Evolution Valid?

Does *The Fourth Day* represent a satisfying resolution of the conflict between the teaching of the Bible and the theory of evolution? Is theistic evolution (or creationomic science) an acceptable position for a serious-minded Christian to take? That is the question we face. A straightforward and emphatic "No" is the answer given to that question in the book *The Great Divide – Christianity OR Evolution* (1988) by Berghoef and DeKoster.[1] For what it is worth let me say that I must share that judgment. I have always had serious doubts about the validity of the theistic evolutionary point of view. My reading and rereading of Van Till's thought-provoking study has reinforced those doubts. Many serious questions are raised by this book. Naturally one who is not a student of Physics and Astronomy can hardly sit in judgment on the professor's opinions in his field of specialized work. However, the book gets into the areas of Biblical interpretation, theology and philosophy, areas of pressing concern for any study of origins among Christians. In these areas I think I have some right to speak.

At the same time one is puzzled by an aspect of Van Till's scientific effort. He seems to be very sure of certain opinions in science, opinions that may well have a considerable amount of contemporary support. But the story of scientific opinion, by common knowledge, is one marked by wide and sharp disagreement. What is hailed as scientifically valid at one time may soon be in for a thorough overhauling or be tossed into science's waste basket. And at any single time one commonly finds as much difference of opinion among scientists as he does among theologians, philosophers and political pundits.

No Room For the Miracle-Working God

How does Van Till look at the universe? He seeks to view the universe as both a scientist and a Christian. His book represents an effort that would take both the Bible and science seriously. Such effort is to be commended. We as a church have a Confession of Faith which declares that God is made known

---

[1]See an extensive review of this book by the present writer in *The Outlook*, Sept. 1988, pp. 21-24.

76

to us through *general* revelation (the created world, nature) and *special* revelation (the Bible). Does Van Till's book succeed in integrating the scientist's observations and conclusions with the teaching of the Bible as that teaching is confessed in the Christian Reformed Church? Is it evident that this student of astronomy and physics reads the "most elegant book" of general revelation under the ruling conviction that God has made himself "more clearly and fully known to us by His Holy and divine Word?" (Confession of Faith, Article II).

From his perspective he sees a magnificent cosmos which displays "patterns of material behavior" that are "spatially and temporally invariant: they are the same everywhere and 'everywhen' " (*The Fourth Day,* p. 116). This judgment is drawn from the study of the stars and other heavenly phenomena, their behavior and their history. Van Till sees in this stellar behavior and history a demonstration of the behavior and history of all the material world. Of this created world he says that it is "a system of material objects presenting empirically observable properties, rigorously patterned behavior, and a coherent temporal development" (*Ibid,* p. 205). The professor declares furthermore, "Because the observed behavior of matter follows very strict patterns which can be precisely described and mathematically represented, we often refer to these patterns, or their mathematical representations, as 'natural laws' " (*Ibid,* p. 221). These rigidly conceived natural processes, we are told, have been going on without variation "everywhere and 'everywhen' " for fifteen billion years, beginning with the so-called "Big Bang."

When we see this orderly cosmos as the scientist sees it, according to Van Till, the universe takes on a certain dependable coherence that allows for no breaks or "discontinuities." These natural processes constitute the "internal affairs" of the cosmos and they are the domain of the scientist. This tightly running cosmic operation can be viewed as having *external relationships,* which are the domain of "philosophy and theology — and thus ultimately of scriptural authority" (*Ibid,* p. 194). "In addition to having questions about the internal intelligibility of the corporeal universe," wrote the Calvin scientist, "we can ask questions about the possibilities and character of its relationship to external, nonmaterial entities, powers and beings" (*Ibid,* p. 195). It would appear that God must be thought of as one, yes, the supreme one, of these "external, nonmaterial entities, powers and beings."

Where is room for God to work miracles in this tight cosmic operation in which natural processes go on invariantly for billions of years, "everywhere and 'everywhen,'" and there can be no breaks or "discontinuities" in these unchanging and unchangeable natural laws? How can God be thought of as intervening in these natural processes when he is described as being "external" to the "internal affairs" of the cosmos? The conclusion seems inescapable that the teaching of Van Till's book does not allow for a miracle-working God, who can, did and does intervene in the natural processes of this world for his redemptive purposes.

This judgment calls for specifics. For illustration we consider the virgin birth of Christ. The womb of Mary of Nazareth was part of the material world, in which all processes function according to unchangeable and unchanging natural laws, according to the findings of "experiential observation." How then could that womb be impregnated by the Holy Spirit, the third person of the God who is defined as being "external" to all natural processes?

Likewise the body of the person Jesus Christ was part of the material world. When that body died after crucifixion, in the manner in which all bodies perish under the rule of the "rigorously patterned behavior" of Van Till's world, it had to decay and eventually return to the dust after this same "rigorously patterned behavior" of the material world. How then can we speak of Christ's bodily resurrection?

Similar questions assail us with respect to Christ's death on the cross, accompanied as it was by phenomena such as the three hours of extraordinary darkness and an earthquake, happenings which marked the death of God's Son in the flesh as a tremendous event of cosmic significance. There is no room for such a nature-rattling event in Van Till's tight natural system, to which God is an outsider.

The problem becomes even more pressing with respect to the incarnation of the Son of God. Under the thinking of this book how is it possible for Christians to hold to the position that the Son of God, that is, God himself in the second person of the Trinity, entered into our flesh to be our Savior? Can chapter one of the gospel of John possibly be true? The argumentation of Van Till literally makes the incarnation of the Son

78

of God a piece of nonsense. Everything in the physical world, including Christ's body, is part of a natural system which operates according to fixed and invariable natural processes or laws. How then could He become part of this system through his incarnation, in a manner that violates the invariability of these natural processes and with God being thought of as "external" to this natural world?

Heavy Ambiguity

By this time a reader of Van Till's book may be ready to scream that the above criticism is unfair. The professor has plainly said, "There is, in other words, no natural process that falls outside the Creator's domain of action" (*Ibid*, p. 223). He also wrote this, "But the Creator of which the Bible speaks is neither temporally nor spatially remote; on the contrary, he acted not only in an instant of origination but at every moment: he is continually active in sustaining and preserving the very existence of that which he originated" (p. 62). Furthermore, he has stated again and again that God is the "Originator, Preserver, Governor and Provider of the Creation" (p. 65 and elsewhere). And, what is more, Van Till has said in just so many words, "As recounted in the Bible, God has often performed miracles – extra-ordinary signs – to reveal his identity as Lord of the universe and Redeemer of his people" (*The Banner*, Oct. 12, 1987, p. 15).

What shall we say to all of this? All we can say at this point is that there is very troublesome ambiguity here. The committee of the Board of Trustees of Calvin College and Seminary that investigated the views of Van Till and his colleagues also found ambiguity in the views of Van Till. (See *Acts of Synod 1988, p. 594*). Can we allow for such troublesome ambiguity in crucial matters of the faith in the declared views of teachers and leaders of the church? We have seen that the Board of Trustees of Dordt College did not think so when they found statements in a professor's syllabus that seemed to contradict what he personally confessed. Should we not expect those who teach our young to express themselves with full clarity in such crucial matters of faith as Christ's incarnation and bodily resurrection, and also creation by God's Word, the creation of man in the image of God, and the fall of man? The Bible defines faith with the words "assurance" and "conviction" (Heb.

11:1). Lord's Day VII of the Heidelberg Catechism, echoing the teaching of the Bible, confesses that "True faith is not only a knowledge and conviction that everything God reveals in his Word is true; it is also deep-rooted assurance . . ." The language of faith speaks with affirmation, not ambiguity.

Van Till correctly wants to avoid indentifying God with the natural process of creation. In other words, he does not want to slip into the pitfall of pantheism. At the same time he wants to avoid deism, which regards the world as running on its own once it had been started by the Creator. Hence, he speaks of God as an "external" being or power who at the same time acts as the "Originator, Preserver, Governor and Provider of the creation."

My problems with this way of thinking are highlighted further when we reflect on the "great commission" of our Lord. When Jesus, risen in victory, gave orders to his disciples to "go and make disciples of all nations," he set in motion all sorts of physical processes that have been going on ever since he gave these marching orders to his church. Countless bodies have moved from continent to continent and to the islands of sea, monies have been gathered, houses and hospitals built, horses and trains and cars and airplanes have been on the move. Was the stirring of all this physical (and spiritual) activity done by a power or being *external* to all the universe's natural processes? And when the Holy Spirit moved and continues to move people to *go*, is this activity by the third person of the divine Trinity an action carried out by a power or force *external* to all the universe's corporeal processes?

Equally to the point is the question whether it is an *external* power or force or entity that activates people to obey the call to do all things to the glory of God, so that they use more electrical power in studying harder, or that they drive their cars more responsibly, or write out a check for the poor, or swing a hammer in building a home for the homeless, or perform one's daily task with more vigor. Is the third person of the holy Trinity an *external* power or entity in activating all these and countless more such movements with their involvement of natural processes?

One has to conclude that Van Till's sharp separation between the *internal affairs* of the world's physical processes and the *external* relationships of this cosmic machine just doesn't hold up. He has not done justice to the complexities of the relationship between God and the physical world, between the spiritual and the natural.

Total Evolution

According to Dr. Van Till this orderly world of natural law and its history are to be understood to form "the intricately designed pattern of cosmic evolution. Spatial evolution, galactic evolution, elemental evolution, stellar evolution, planetary evolution, and biological evolution are coherently integrated and intertwining processes that serve as the individual threads in the tapestry: the dynamic order of patterned development marks the whole of cosmic history" (*Ibid*, p. 254). Man himself, we are told, evolved in this universal process of "coherently related patterns of material behavior." The argument for total evolution proceeds as we read this, "To consider the possibility that we are creatures (members of God's Creation) whose capacity for the awareness of self, of God, and of our responsibility for obedience to divine mandates has been formed through a process of continuous evolutionary development does not strike me as inappropriate or incongruous or unbiblical. I see no reason whatsoever to deny that the Creation might have an evolutionary history or that morally responsible creatures might have been formed through the processes of evolutionary development" (*Ibid*, p. 258).

This teaching of total evolutionism is an effort at combining the teaching of the Bible with the insights gleaned from a particular area of scientific study. In evaluating this teaching we must take note of what Van Till means by Creation. The word creation is used to refer to the whole magnificent orderly cosmos of which man is also a part. In other words, the creation is what God created. However, when the word is used in speaking of God's work of Creation, Van Till departs from the usual understanding of the word. He says he does not object to the statement "The cosmos *was* created by God." But he prefers to say "The cosmos *is* God's Creation" (p. 66). He prefers not to use the word Creation for that work of God whereby he formed the world and all that is in it at some past point in time. For Van Till Creation is God's continuing activity through the natural processes which are open to human observation and scientific analysis. God is called, we have seen, the

Originator, Preserver, Governor and Provider of the Creation. For Van Till these titles describe God as the Creator. They represent "the multiple categories of divine creativity." (See *ibid,* pp. 61ff.). We are told that God's work of origination (called *exnihilation,* that is, creation ex nihilo, creation out of nothing) is in a class by itself, for it is beyond human experience and observation. For this reason God's work as Originator of the cosmos is not meaningful to the scientist, who works with "experiential observation."

All of this is thoroughly mystifying. How are we to understand this creativity of God as Preserver, Governor and Provider when the Creation is described as a fixed system of invariant natural processes that have been going on for fifteen billion years, a system allowing for no "discontinuities?" God cannot act with free creativity, as we have seen earlier in this chapter in our discussion of some of the great acts of God in redemptive history. To act creatively is to produce something new and fresh, something different from what already is (Heb. 11:3). God is not sovereignly free to act creatively in accordance with his perfect wisdom and power, since it seems inescapable that He himself is limited by an invariant system of natural laws. Despite his intent to avoid deistic ways of thinking, it seems to me that Van Till has slipped into such a view of God and the world.

Unbiblical and Unconfessional

Van Till's ideas on Creation have to be labeled unbiblical and unconfessional. Has the Christian church ever understood God's work of creation to be anything other than a work taking place "in the beginning" over a period of time ("six days")? This act of creation is related by Van Till to God as Originator, and this is limited to exnihilation, which at one point he speaks of as "an instant of origination" (*Ibid,* p. 62). Surely there is marked discrepancy here between the professor's views and the church's consistent confession. He sees Creation as process of evolution. So he speaks much of Creation and means thereby a continuing process covering billions of years and controlled always by the Creator acting as Preserver, Governor and Provider. He puts his own particular meaning into the first words of the Apostles' Creed and can say with the appearance of orthodoxy, "And with these words we lay the foundation for all the Christian faith. If God were not our Maker, by what authority could he offer to be our Redeemer?" (*The Banner*, Sept. 28, 1987, p. 16). (The final clause of that quotation invites comment, but I refrain).

The past tense in the statement "The cosmos was created by God" is not satisfactory to Van Till. When one examines the Bible carefully he finds that it is precisely the past tense that is used repeatedly when God's work of creation is spoken of. Besides the record of Genesis 1 and 2 the past tense is used in the following passages of Scripture: Psalm 33:6, 9; Psalm 90:2, Psalm 96:5, Psalm 102:25, Psalm 148:5, Isaiah 40:26, 28; Isaiah 42:5, Isaiah 45:18, Jeremiah 10:12, John 1:3, Acts 14:15, Acts 17:24, Colossians 1:16, Revelation 4:11, Revelation 10:6. Especially relevant are the words of Nehemiah 9:6 – "You alone are the Lord. You made the heavens, even the highest heavens, and all their starry host, the earth and all that is on it, the seas and all that is in them. You give life to everything, and the multitudes of heaven worship you." The words "you give life to everything" (NIV) are more familiar to many in the rendering of the Revised Standard Version, namely, "thou preservest all of them" (see also KJV).

Particularly impressive is the disparity between Van Till's formulation and the teaching of the church's confessions. Article XII of the Confession of Faith reads in part as follows: "We believe that the Father by the Word, that is, by His Son, has created of nothing the heaven, the earth, and all creatures, when it seemed good unto Him, giving unto every creature its being, shape, form and several offices to serve its Creator; that He also upholds and governs them by His eternal providence and infinite power for the service of mankind, to the end that man may serve his God."

Question-Answer 26 of the Heidelberg Catechism asks the question, "What do you believe when you say: 'I believe in God, the Father, Almighty, Maker of heaven and earth?' " The answer in part is, "That the eternal Father of our Lord Jesus Christ, who of nothing made heaven and earth with all that is in them, who likewise upholds and governs the same by His eternal counsel and providence, is for the sake of Christ His son my God and my Father."

Creation And Providence

Van Till's ideas regarding creation and providence (packaged together under God's continuing Creation) constitute a marked revision of Reformed thinking in the interest of his evolutionary scheme. Obviously he could not argue for his evolutionary system with a show of respect for Biblical teaching if God's work of creation were thought of in the traditional confessional manner. Man owes his being, character and continuing existence to God the Creator and to him alone, both because he formed that life in the first place and because He continues to preserve and govern it. This cluster of ideas shines brightly in the speech that the apostle Paul made to the questioning Greeks of the Areopagus. Paul would have his hearers come to know the true God, the Unknown God of the Athenians. The apostle introduced God as the Creator first of all, "the God who made the world and everything in it." Then the apostle spoke of the God of providence who "gives all men life and breath and everything else." This God, who wants men to know him and to serve him, is the key to life, for "in him we live, and move and have our being" (Acts 17:22-28).

Why is it important to preserve the distinction between God's work of creation and that of his providence? They are, of course, closely related, for both have to do with God's relationship to the created world. But they must be viewed as distinct, and that for at least two reasons.

The first reason is that in his work of creation God acted in majestic and solitary sovereignty. There simply was nothing else that could in any way have a part in the creation of all things. He created it all "of nothing," as our confessions say. He and he alone, as the triune God, was involved in the work of creation. The created world took on its being, character and wondrous variety from the infinite wisdom and power of the Creator alone.

It is not so with the providential preservation and government of the created world. After God's work of creation was done a very different situation was in place. Now there was in existence a marvelous world that had a reality distinct from that of God. Now God in his perfect wisdom makes use of secondary causes in the care and management of the world he made. This is especially true when we consider the place of God's image-bearer. God gave him high position in the created world. He gave man a "cultural mandate," calling upon him to rule over the rest of creation for God and with Him. God gave to man great gifts in order that he might properly discharge this high office. God's providential government of the creation reckons with and uses the capacities and gifts of his creatures to the glory of His name and well-being of His creation. This important element of God's government of the world marks his providence as a distinct divine work. Seeing this point in all of its rich meaningfulness prompts amazement and gratitude at the place of dignity given especially to man, the creature bearing the very image of God.

When we compare the line of thinking outlined in the preceding paragraphs with that set forth in Van Till's book, it becomes apparent that the two sets of ideas are far apart. Van Till sees the created world as a complex of "natural processes" that have been going on for billions of years and that can allow for no variation or "discontinuities." In relation to this tight system of "natural law" God is an "external non-material entity, power or being." God is said to be the "Originator, Preserver, Governor and Provider of the creation." These titles have little more than verbal significance in the government of Van Till's tight cosmic machine. It seems to me that this kind of thinking dishonors both God and man. When we recognize God as actively involved in the affairs of the universe that is his because he made it, then we accord to God the honor that is his due. And when we see man as God's appointed co-worker in the world, then his place is one of dignity and high responsibility. In an evolutionary scheme he has neither dignity nor high responsibility.

A second reason why we must preserve the distinction between God's works of creation and providence is that by doing so we avoid deistic and pantheistic ways of thinking. When we do justice to God's distinct work of providence in preserving and governing the world he made, we avoid thinking of the created world as a machine that runs on its own by the laws of God originally established. When we do justice to God's distinct work of creation we avoid thinking of the universe and everything in it as in any way identifiable with God.

"Primeval History"

More troublesome problems arise in Van Till's evolutionary understanding of Biblical teaching. Many of these problems come with his contention that the first eleven chapters of Genesis do not constitute "actual history" but rather "primeval history" (*Ibid*, pp. 80ff.). He likens such history to a parable. In both "the concrete details of the story constitute the packaging in which . . . truth is conveyed." Then he adds this comment: "the content of truth is of infinitely greater value than the vehicle or packaging in which it is carried."

Where do we go with this distinction between truth and packaging? Did Jesus and Paul make this distinction when they referred to persons and events appearing in Genesis 1-11? Who determines how this kind of thinking is to be applied to specific instances? Van Till tells us how he applies this distinction in the understanding of Genesis 1. Bearing in mind Van Till's ideas respecting God's work of Creation, we read as follows, "The seven-day chronology that we find in Genesis 1 has no connection with the actual chronology of the Creator's continuous dynamic action in the cosmos. The creation-week motif is a literary device, a framework in which a number of very important messages are held. The chronology of the narrative is not the chronology of but rather the packaging in which the message is wrapped. The particular acts depicted in the Story of the Creator are not the events of creative action reported with photographic realism but rather imaginative illustrations of the way in which God and the Creation are related" (*Ibid*, pp. 84f.).

Much of the force of this statement is taken away when we recall and reject Van Till's own special ideas of Creation, as evaluated previously. Furthermore, there is a literary factor that bears on our understanding of Genesis 1, but Van Till goes too far when he speaks of the creation–week motif as a literary device that is no more than packaging for what he sees as the real message to be conveyed. And' it seems appropriate to ask whose imagination he is talking about – that of Moses, that of the Holy Spirit, or his own.

What About Adam?

To accept Van Till's notion of primeval history in his evolutionary scheme is to face serious questions regarding several other important elements of the Christian faith. The many overtures that came to Synod 1988 regarding this whole matter raised these questions. I quote from one of these overtures, one addressing itself to the report of the Board committee that evaluated the views of the three professors, with special reference to the evolutionary ideas of Van Till and Menninga.

1. The only man we know in the Scriptures and in the creeds is one who from the beginning of his creaturely existence was equipped with full competence for morally responsible action, for "God created man good and in his own image, that is, in true righteousness and holiness . . ." (Heidelberg Catechism III, 6; see also Confession of Faith, Article XIV). There simply is no place in the Scriptures or the creeds for a view of man that says "morally responsible creatures might have been formed through the processes of evolutionary development."

2. The Biblical and creedal teaching of man's creation in the image of God is jeopardized when it is allowed that man's creation could have occurred by "the processes of evolutionary development." At what point did the image of God begin to appear in a creation process covering millions of years? Is the image of God divisible or developmental, with the image of God meaning full capacity to act in moral responsibility? Is the name Adam to be given to all the slowly developing creatures that began to take on human characteristics over eons of time? Of these slowly developing creatures, which one first bore the image of God as defined in the creeds?

3. The related teachings of the fall of man and of original sin are also jeopardized in such evolutionary theories. The moral conduct of Adam was filled with dire consequences for all manRind. (See Romans 5:12-19; Confession of Faith Articles XIV, XV; Heidelberg Catechism II-7, IV-9; Canons of Dort I, Article 1, and III-IV, Articles 1,2,3.) The Bible and the creeds clearly teach that the one man Adam created by God plunged the human race into sin. What man did this if we construe man's creation as taking place by means of evolutionary development over unknown eons of time?

4. The efforts of these professors to seek to explain God's work of creation by means of their "scientific theories" of evolutionary development cannot be harmonized with the teaching of Hebrews 11:3, where we read as follows: "By faith we understand that the universe was formed at God's command, so that what is seen was not made out of what was visible."[2]

---

[2]See *Acts of Synod 1988*, pp. 435-436.

Our Confidence

In pondering the evolutionary teaching we have been examining one is struck by the confidence Professor Van Till has in the constancy of natural processes through billions of years. He says this constancy gives to the universe a *coherence* that gives meaning to the scientific endeavor and intelligibility to the material world. More than that, such constancy serves as a "fitting context" for human responsibility (pp. 257f.), and is an important ingredient in the evolutionary teaching that will give to today's children a solid, respectable foundation for a God-glorifying life (see pp. 263ff.).

What shall we think of determinations made about natural processes that occurred fifteen billion years ago? No scientist observed what happened then. So Van Till makes decisions about what happened in the far, far distant past by means of an accumulation of scientific observations together with uniformatarian thinking, mathematical extrapolation,[3] and a number of critical assumptions. No brash negativism regarding scientific activity or mathematical computation is in order in today's world of scientific achievement. However, may we assume that natural processes observed today are precisely the same as those that took place billions of years ago? May we make the kind of leap that Van Till makes when he moves from stellar evolution to human evolution? Shall we likewise put our confidence in such a scheme built with the materials of experiential observation, uniformitarianism, mathematical extrapolation and critical assumptions?

We cannot find our confidence there. We respect the scientist's awed sense of the lawfulness of the universe. We respect his effort to take both science and the Bible seriously. But – our confidence is in God, the God who created us in his image by his wondrous Word, the God who has made us a "new creation" in Christ by the mysterious power of the Spirit, the God who one day will terminate natural processes and make a wholly new creation. And his creating Word will reign supreme.

---

[3]A dictionary definition of the word *extrapolate* is "To infer or estimate (unknown information) from known information." Hence, talk about numerical values in the billions is to extrapolate numerical values we know and understand to numerical values we don't know and understand.

It is our faith in this great God of truth, wisdom and love that gives us full confidence (also in nature's lawfulness), that invests our lives with profound moral character, and that fills us with the great riches of a salvation that makes everything new.

The Days Of Creation

There is one facet of this whole matter of origins that deserves special attention. It has to do with the "days" of creation. What are we to think of those "days" mentioned in Genesis 1 and 2, the six days in which God created the world and the seventh day on which he rested from his work? Are we to understand the Bible to say that they were regular twenty-four solar days as we know them? Or are we to think of them as long periods of time, as some teach? Is there another alternative? How are we to understand the Bible's teaching on this question?

That is the question, of course. Our approach to this question should be strictly exegetical, not speculative. It should be punctually observed that the question is not what we think God *could* have done in an instant of time or in any measure of time.

If we want to be strictly Biblical in this matter, are we then not committed to the position that creation took place in six regular days of twenty-four hours each? This is a common opinion among Christians, and anyone who thinks differently on the subject is often viewed with suspicion. Creation in six regular calendar days seems to be the prevailing opinion among Christians. Berkhof presents this view very well in his *Systematic Theology* (pp. 153ff.).

It should be noted, on the other hand, that throughout the history of the Christian church there have been those who took a different view. Augustine, for instance, believed that God created all things in an instant, and that the days of Genesis 1 are not intended to serve as a temporal order of creation, but rather to present the causal relationship that existed among the various parts of creation.

In more modern times scholars of repute among Reformed people have held differing views of the days of creation. Herman Bavinck regarded the first three creation days as "special cosmic days," not days as we know them. In fact, he argued that all the creation days were such cosmic units, "God's

89

workdays," in which He prepared the entire earth and changed chaos into cosmos.[4]

Charles Hodge came to the opinion that the teaching of Scripture and the findings of science could best be harmonized by viewing the days of creation as periods of time in indefinite duration.[5] William G. T. Shedd argued that "there is nothing in the use of the word 'day' by Moses that requires it to be explained as invariably denoting a period of twenty-four hours, but much to forbid it."[6] More recently G. Ch. Aadlers of The Netherlands has asserted that the idea that the creation days were 24-hour periods of time "is certainly without any substantiation in Scripture."[7] Also, the solidly Biblical scholar E. J. Young has declared that "the first three days are not solar days such as we now know." He says further, "The Hebrew word *yom* is much like our English word *day*, and it is capable of a great number of connotations."[8]

A study of the word *day* is fascinating and instructive. It is plain that in Genesis 1 the Hebrew Bible uses the word day to mean or denote first of all a set period of time, since evening and morning are mentioned in each instance. But when we turn to Genesis 2 we immediately see a change in the use of the word day. Here the whole of the work of creation is in view, and the King James version renders the sense literally and correctly when it says, "in the day that the Lord made the earth and the heavens."[9] We have the same broader connotation of the word day in Genesis 2:17, where we read the warning regarding the tree of the knowlege of good and evil

---

[4]Bavinck, *Gereformeerde Dogmatiek* II, pp. 530-534.

[5]C. Hodge, *Systematic Theology* I, pp. 570-571.

[6]W. G. T. Shedd, *Dogmatic Theology I*, p. 476.

[7]G. Ch. Aalders, *Genesis, Vol I*, c1981, p. 58. In *Bible Student's Commentary*. This commentary series is an English translation of the highly regarded Dutch *Korte Verklaring Der Heilige Schrift*, which originally appeared in the thirties, forties and fifties. Aalders' full commentary at this point is well worth reading.

[8]E. J. Young, *In The Beginning*, c. 1976, p. 43.

[9]The NIV loses this point when it renders the clause as "when the Lord God made the earth and the heaven," though this reading is wholly acceptable in the light of our understanding of the word day.

in these words, "in the day you eat of it you will surely die." The warning does not necessarily mean that man will die within a twenty-four period after eating from the tree. It seems obvious that the warning means in the *event* you eat of it. Thus the New International Version can translate the passage with the words "when you eat of it."

So from the very beginning of God's written revelation we have a development in the use of the word day that moves from day as a set measure of time to day as a vehicle for an event or cluster of events. Day and event are most intimately related. An event happens in time, and day is the measure of time. Hence there are many references in the Bible to day as a set period (of twenty-four hours or just the daylight hours). On the other hand the word day referring to event or time or occasion appears again and again in the writings of Moses and throughout Scripture. In Genesis 35:3 Jacob speaks of "the day of my distress" in referring to his flight from the anger of Esau. In Deuteronomy 32:35 God through Moses warns of judgment on sinful Israel as "the day of their calamity." In many other passages the word day is used to refer to time generally, that is, as the occasion of some event or development, as in the frequently used expressions "on that day" and "to that day." When we move to the other end of the time spectrum we meet the same use of the word day in the references to the Judgment Day, or simply "that day." Clearly such references relate to the final judgment event and not to a particular twenty-four hour period of time. And the same kind of usage persists *to our own day. In our day* we have a comparable usage in the expression *moment of truth*. Another comparable usage is found in the words of Winston Churchill when he described the splendid stand of the English people under the intense bombing of World War II with the words "their finest hour."

Thus the word *day* first of all denotes a period of time of twenty-four hours. The day is the common measure of time. Events happen in time. Therefore the word day can mean or represent event. Hence I see no good reason to insist that the days of Genesis 1 and 2 are twenty-four hour periods. Genesis 1, by the use of the word day, lays out for us a series of creation events done by the Word and power of the great Creator God. How much elapsed time he used to perform these creation events, we do not know. Unlike his creatures, God is not time-bound (II Peter 3:8). The account in Genesis 1 plainly tells us that God created the world by his Word of power and wisdom. That Word of power and wisdom was in actuality Jesus Christ, the second person of the Trinity, as the Bible teaches in John 1:1-3, "In the beginning was the Word"—the Word of truth, the Word of order, the Word of creation, the Word that would one day be the historical Word of Redemption for this creation. (See also Col. 1:15-20).

Genesis 1 teaches us that God in a series of creative acts or events formed the world and everything in it. These six "days" came to their climax in the creation of God's image-bearer who would govern the world as God's vicegerent (Gen. 1:26-28). Some students of the Bible take the position that the order of the events as given in Genesis 1 should be rearranged to meet objections such as those involving the appearance of the sun on the fourth day. I see no pressing exegetical reason for such rearrangement.

What should be clear is that when we see the days of Genesis 1 as meaning or representing God's creation events, we are not thereby endorsing the notion that these days are long periods of time. All such notions go beyond what the Bible teaches and are therefore speculative. The language of faith is neither that of ambiguity nor speculation, but rather that of affirmation. However, when we understand Genesis 1 in the manner here outlined, the scientist who would do justice to what the Bible teaches gains some elbow room for his reflections on the data he discovers in his area of study. We give him some relief from the rigidity that attends the belief that the days of creation must be viewed as being twenty-four hour periods of time. At the same time let it be said that the opinions here expressed on the days of Genesis 1 and 2 do not, in the mind of the writer, constitute a first step toward the adoption of an evolutionary point of view.

Two Final Observations

Does not the language of the fourth commandment in Exodus 20:11 require that we regard the creation days in Genesis 1 as twenty-four hour periods of time? It would seem so. However, the very point of our discussion lies right here. The days of Genesis 1 refer, first of all, to twenty-four hour periods of time, though Moses was using the word day proleptically with the first three days, since the sun did not appear until the fourth day. But these very days became the vehicle for conveying the events of the creative works of God. The flexibility of the word day is present in the fourth commandment. Moses, the author of both Genesis 1 and Exodus 20, could use the word day to mean a twenty-four hour period of time, and he could at another point use the word to represent events that happen in time. There is no real conflict. Furthermore, there is a question with regard to the fourth commandment with its reference to the seventh day, the day of God's rest. Was God's "sabbath" from the work of creation limited to twenty-four hours? Does not this question lend support to the position that the word day in the account of creation represents creation event? It seems highly improper to assign a specific duration time to the seventh day. The point that stands out in the seventh day is the event of God's rest.

Evolution In The Christian Schools?

Our second final observation touches on Van Till's concern for the teaching of "creationomic science" in the Christian schools. Should these evolutionary views be taught to our children? If Van Till's ideas of creation and evolution are to be taught in the Christian schools, ruinous pedagogical and spiritual woes must inevitably follow. The critical flaws we see in the professor's understanding of origins simply cannot be taught in the classroom without bringing in their train serious problems with regard to the teaching of the Bible at many points, as earlier discussions have tried to demonstrate.

Let the Christian school teacher present the story of creation as that is given in the Bible. At that stage when the student is ready for more mature study let the teacher open up to him the conception of the days of creation that sees these days as representing the creation events recorded in Genesis 1 and 2. Since such teaching would always be working straightforwardly with Biblical data devoid of speculative elements, pedagogical or spiritual difficulties could hardly arise. On the other hand, serious trouble will be incurred when the teacher tries to explain the difference between primeval history and textbook history, with the extensive revision of Biblical teaching that this distinction entails.

The teaching of creation is of basic and crucial importance in the life of a covenant child. His whole life is anchored in the words "In the beginning God created the heavens and the earth." These words, as explained further in Genesis 1 and 2, form the beginning of a spiritual pilgrimage in which every experience and every contact with the rich, colorful tapestry of nature will draw him into closer fellowship with that glorious God in whom "we live and move and have our being." This God is not some force or being external to the cosmic machine we are part of. Rather He who made it all and governs it all is our God, our strength and our hope, day by day, hour by hour. Let nothing taught in the classroom of a *Christian* school rob precious children of that anchorage of life.

CHAPTER 8

More Marks of a Church in Trouble

A word that has surfaced many times in the previous chapters is the word *confusion*. It has been pointed out on numerous occasions that some development in the church, some decision, some committee report, or some way of handling an issue has not contributed to a clearer understanding and witness on the part of the church, but has contributed rather to confusion and uncertainty. Any number of times in recent years I have heard statements like this, "We don't seem to know where we stand anymore." It hardly needs saying that such confusion and uncertainty cannot fail to make for a decline in the vitality and witness of the church. Also resulting is a growing lack of a sense of direction. The Apostle John admonished the church in Philadelphia to "Hold fast what you have." When a church's sense of Biblical and confessional direction begins to fade, it can hardly maintain a firm grip on what it has received. A symptom of this slippage is the astonishing ease with which Christian Reformed members drift away to join other communions where often the Reformed vision of life is largely or wholly absent.

In this chapter I wish to explore a number of other areas where this confusion and uncertainty are evident. One such area is the prolonged engagement of the church with the issue of women in office.

The Bible and the Women-in-Office Issue

This engagement covered a period of about twenty years and involved six different synodical committees. A helpful summary of the history of this debate appeared in *The Banner* of April 17, 1989.

This protracted history with its many different study committees tells its own story of a church resistant to opening the special offices in the church to women. In 1978 the Synod acted to open the office of deacon to women. But the decision was made even though there was clear evidence that a majority of the members of the Christian Reformed Church were opposed to opening the offices to women. Why this opposition? Tradition? Very likely in some measure. But the main reason clearly seemed to be that in the minds of this majority the Bible limits these offices to men. And this is why action taken by the Synod of 1975 was very much in line with the thinking of the church. Synod 1975 decided that the practice of excluding women from the special offices (pastor, elder, deacon – and later evangelist) "be maintained unless compelling Biblical grounds are advanced for changing the practice" (*Acts of Synod 1975*, p. 78). This decision showed due regard for the history and integrity of the Christian church as well as for the teaching of the Bible.

That was the key issue in the debate – what does the Bible teach on this score? It is not a question of ability on the part of women to serve. It is not a question of what you or I might like to see happen. No doubt there are women who are well equipped to render acceptable services in these offices. This is especially true of the office of deacon. Women generally are endowed with gifts and traits of character that equip them admirably for many types of diaconal work, and the church should use these gifts.

But the Christian Reformed Church has a problem in making use of these good gifts in the office of deacon as that office is maintained in this communion. This is a problem our Presbyterian friends do not have. Even very conservative Presbyterian churches have women serving as deacons. However, in these churches deacons do not sit on the governing body of the congregation, that is, on the session. In the Christian Reformed Church deacons sit on the church council and therefore in some measure participate in the government of the church. This is the sticking point. It is clear to a large number of the members of the church that the Bible forbids a woman to hold a position in the church in which she rules over a man. So, there is little unwillingness to use the good gifts women have for diaconal service. Most, one suspects, would want to make good use of these fine gifts, but only in a setting that does not violate what seems to many to be the plain teaching of the Scripture.

The teaching of the Bible is the church's supreme and only infallible rule of faith and practice. One finds it hard to believe that scripture ruled in the decision of 1978 to open the office of deacon to women. The passages in the Bible that were appealed to in support of the decision were clearly relevant only to those who wanted such relevance. Such passages were Romans 16:1, Galatians 3:28 and I Timothy 3:11.

In the ongoing debate over women in ecclesiastical office confusion is further compounded by claims to the effect that opening the offices to women is a sign of the Holy Spirit's leading of the church into a new era. Does the Holy Spirit lead the church into ways of doing its work that are at variance with the teaching of the Bible? By what warrant does one claim that some new development is the work of the Holy Spirit? Surely such warrant has to be more than the opinion of a person or a group of persons. Is it possible that the appeal to the leading of the Holy Spirit in such situations is little more than a pious effort to achieve some objective when clear Biblical support for such objective is lacking.

Also adding to the confusion is the appeal by some to the cultural conditioning of the Bible. There is evidence of such cultural conditioning in the Bible, of course. The frequent usage of language reflecting a pastoral way of life is such evidence, for example. The place of the Roman empire in the unfolding history of the New Testament is another such piece of evidence of cultural and historical conditioning. Awareness of such conditioning helps to illuminate the teaching of the Bible. But this can be a treacherous area for the Bible student, as an overture from Classis Florida to Synod 1985 indicated (see chapter 6). To view the Bible as a time-bound or culture-bound book is to undercut its character as the unchanging and ever-relevant Word of God. The Bible reflects cultural influences, but the Word of God transcends such cultural limitations. It shall stand "forever."[1]

Concerned Members

Many members of the Christian Reformed Church are concerned about the state of the denomination they love. This

---

[1]For further commentary on the women-in-office issue see Appendix B.

remark is not only about the group known as the Committee of the Concerned Members. There are many members of the church not connected with this Committee who are troubled about trends in the Christian Reformed Church. As a matter of fact, at the time of this writing there are no less than six groupings of members who are in varying ways and degrees dissatisfied with the state of affairs in the Christian Reformed Church. They are the Reformed Fellowship (publishers for some forty years of *The Outlook*), Mid-American Reformed Seminary, the Consistorial Conference (located in the Midwest), the *Christian Renewal* magazine, the developing Christian Reformed Alliance (based in Ontario), in addition to the Committee of Concerned Members. And there are concerned members who are part of none of these groupings.

This item is mentioned for two reasons. In the first place, these facts should alert the entire membership of the Christian Reformed Church. The presence in the fellowship of so many people who are much concerned over developments in the church should be cause for sober reflection on the part of all. When there is real concern for the well-being of a member of a family, all members of the family generally take a serious view of such concern. It seems to be only good sense for the Christian Reformed Church as a whole to be exercised about the presence of so many concerned members in its midst. And may God forbid that there could be those in the church who adopt the attitude that says, "We have the votes; let those concerned people pout."

Closely related to the preceding is a second reason why so much concern in the church should be taken seriously by all. It has been patent for some time that there are those who look upon their concerned brothers and sisters with something less than respect. In fact, some in the church tend to revile those concerned members as unthinking or narrow-minded troublemakers who ought to fold their tents and silently steal away in the night.

Such attitudes are puzzling. Indeed, they are unChristian. When brothers and sisters in Christ have a troubling concern, such concern should be viewed sympathetically by others in the church. "Weep with those who weep" (Rom. 12:15. Romans 12 and I Corinthians 12 make good reading in this connection).

This is especially the case because for the most part these concerned people are devoted members of the body of Christ who love the Bible and want to be true to the Word of God and the Confessions. Oh yes, at times such concerned people can overstate their case. Sometimes their opinions could stand some enlightenment. But in the main they are solid, loyal members of the church.

To those who speak ill of these concerned members I would ask some questions. What kind of members do you want in the church? Do you want members whose allegiance to the Bible and the church is superficial, lacking in depth and meaningful commitment? Do you want the church to become another so-called mainline church whose members are often delightful to meet but who so frequently know next to nothing about what the church stands for? Do you want members who do little thinking for themselves and are willing to let others do their thinking for them? Don't you want members who are strongly committed to the great Reformation principle of the universal priesthood of believers and whose robust stand for the Reformed faith is an invaluable resource for the church of Jesus Christ?

That New Seminary

In September of 1982 something happened in the Christian Reformed Church that was startling to most of the membership of the church. It was then that Mid-America Reformed Seminary opened its doors in northwest Iowa. A number of ministers in the denomination, some of whom had held prominent leadership positions in the church, decided that conditions had reached such a point in the Christian Reformed Church that a new training school for ministers was called for, a school independent of official church control. Many people in the church were shocked at this radical step. The Christian Reformed Church has had a long love affair with "onze school" in Grand Rapids. The appearance of the new school was greeted by disbelief on the part of many, and by scorn and even outrage on the part of others.

Why did the new school happen? A pamphlet put out by the seminary explains as follows—

Why this new seminary? That's the question that naturally presses itself upon us. From the great interest that this new school has stirred and the broad and ardent support it has gained, it is clear that this development is meeting certain needs and desires of the church membership. What are these needs and desires?

For some time we have witnessed a high level of frustration in the church on a number of counts. A common complaint among Christian Reformed worshippers has been that they hardly recognize the worship services as being Christian Reformed. Lack of solid and thorough exegesis of the Word, absence of catechism preaching, trivializing of worship services by all sorts of whimsical and even inane innovations, a scaling down of the place of God's holy law in the services, lack of clear-cut Reformed emphasis in the preaching—these are some of the complaints that are frequently aired by Christian Reformed church members. Visitors at churches where Biblical and confessionally sound preaching were regularly heard have often declared, "We don't hear preaching like that anymore."[2]

The existence of the new seminary raises some important questions for the church. Is the new institution a qualified school for the training of ministers? Who is the judge of that? A consistory looking for a pastor? A classis? Or is the synod or an agent of synod, alone qualified to judge that? Whose task is it to determine whether a graduate of the new school is qualified to be a candidate for the ministry in the Christian Reformed Church? Is the Board of Trustees of Calvin College and Seminary alone capable of making this judgment? Cannot a classis, upon thorough, synodically prescribed examination and with the concurring advice of Synodical Deputies, make that decision?

Must not the question be pushed just a bit further? What is the task of the Board of Trustees of Calvin Seminary (speaking now only of half of its responsibility)? Its task is to maintain a theological school which furnishes an excellent education and training for future ministers in the Christian Reformed Church. The task of examining whether the graduates of the school are qualified to be ministers belongs to the church, the institutional church. The church assigned this task to the Board

---

[2]From the pamphlet entitled *A Vision Renewed.*

as a matter of convenience. And when all the men aspiring to be ministers in the Christian Reformed Church were graduates of Calvin Seminary, that expedient procedure made some sense. But now there is another seminary founded on the same principles as those on which Calvin Seminary is founded except that it is independent of denominational control. Should not the church re-examine its procedure?

That brings up a related question. Should the church continue to insist that all candidates for the ministry must attend Calvin Seminary for one year, preferably the last year? This requirement came into being at a time when students were seeking candidacy after getting their seminary training at schools whose Reformed credentials were open to serious question. Does that consideration apply to Mid-America Reformed Seminary? And if there are those who think the schooling at the new seminary is so inferior that this added year at Calvin Seminary is required, then the question arises whether that one added year will make up for the presumed inferiority. The proof of the pudding is in the eating. Let the church hear and let the church examine its aspiring preachers, and let the schools where these pastors are trained furnish them the best possible education. That is the way the church does its business. This is the way a rather large segment of the church sees these issues, and they have the right to expect a fair hearing. Tensions will grow if these legitimate concerns continue to receive a cool reception from a church too set in its ways to listen.

Ecumenical Adventurism

The Christian Reformed Church is a confessional church, not only formally in the sense that it has creeds, but also actually in the sense that it seeks to preach the Word of God and do its business as a church according to the teaching of the Bible as that is formulated in the confessions. The church may preach nothing nor do anything that compromises these confessions or undermines their controlling role in the life of the church and of its members.

These principles hold true also in the area of ecumenism. In its relationship with other communions the confessional stance and loyalty of the Christian Reformed Church must ever be maintained, never downplayed or weakened. Therefore the church has steadfastly refrained from seeking membership in the National Council of Churches and the World Council of Churches.[3] After an eight-year relationship (1943-51) with the National Association of Evangelicals the church terminated its membership for reasons given in a letter of withdrawal, which said among other things, "It was felt that the testimony the Christian Reformed Church is called to bring in this day and in this world is in danger of being weakened by continued membership in the National Association of Evangelicals" (*Agenda for Synod 1987*, p. 179). The church decided to rejoin the organization in 1988. Probably having some bearing on the decision to rejoin was the fact that the Reformed Presbyterian Church of North America (Covenanter) and the Presbyterian Church in America are members of the Association, and that Dr. John White, a leading and able figure in the RPCNA, became president of the organization in 1988 after serving as first vice-president.

In 1988 the Christian Reformed Church decided against membership in the World Alliance of Reformed Churches. A recommendation to join came before synod from the Interchurch Relations Committee. The decision not to join was dictated in part by the fact that the word Reformed in the name of the Alliance is used very loosely. Many churches in the Alliance may have been Reformed at some point in their history but cannot be called that today in any meaningful sense of the word. Then there are thoroughly liberal churches among the members, such as the Presbyterian Church U.S.A., the United Church of Canada, and the United Church of Christ U.S.A. It is most interesting to see the name of the Remonstrant Brotherhood of the Netherlands on the membership list.

The constitution of the World Alliance of Reformed Churches calls upon the member churches to "recognize that the Reformed tradition is a Biblical, evangelical and doctrinal ethos, rather than any narrow and exclusive definition of faith and order." Dr. Marten Woudstra, Professor Emeritus of Calvin Seminary, has served the church well in alerting it to the real character of the World Alliance. He had this to say about the above

---

[3]The Christian Reformed Church did not hold membership in the Federal Council of Churches for a brief period of six years (1918-24). The Federal Council became the National Council of Churches.

quotation for the constitution of the Alliance, "The WARC says that the Reformed tradition (read: the Reformed confessions) is an 'ethos' and that one should therefore *not* appeal to the confessions' 'narrow' and 'exclusive' definitions as he seeks to accomplish the Alliance goals together with the other allies. This is completely contradictory to the terms of the Form of Subscription, which calls on all office bearers to diligently teach the Reformed doctrines and to *oppose* and *refute* all that militates against them. If we should ever join WARC we would be saying one thing in Grand Rapids, but quite the opposite thing in Geneva, where WARC has its headquarters."[4]

How could a committee (the Interchurch Relations Committee) of the Christian Reformed Church possibly recommend membership in such an organization? In seeking to answer that puzzling question we have to take a look at the history of this committee over the past decade or more. This committee has somehow managed to maintain a membership that is very much of one mind on ecumenical matters. It was refreshing to notice that one member of the committee (Rev. Gerard Bouma) did not agree with the recommendation to join the WARC.[5] It is high time that the church did something to correct the imbalance that has existed on this committee. Its consistently stacked membership has not reflected the thinking of the church. In the article referred to above Woudstra informs us that two people who have for some time been leading figures on the Interchurch Relations Committee are on record as holding that the Christian Reformed Church could join the World Council of Churches without compromising the biblical, Reformed principles of the denomination.

In 1987 the Christian Reformed Church adopted an Ecumenical Charter, a project recommended by the Interchurch Relations Committee in 1985. One of three overtures relating

---

[4]*The Outlook,* June 1988, p. 12.

[5]Bouma's reason for opposing membership was in part as follows: "The CRC ought to abstain from membership as long as WARC admits on an equal basis into its membership churches where denial of the faithful proclamation of the Word of God is not militated against, and where denials of some of the most basic and crucial doctrines of Christianity are tolerated" (*Agenda for Synod 1988,* p. 120).

to the Charter submitted in 1987 called attention to "a great deal of ambiguous, imprecise and hesitant language" in the proposed document. Another overture said the Charter was "vague and imprecise at crucial points" (*Agenda for Synod 1987*, pp. 451-52). The editor of *The Banner* wrote, ". . . the charter is unclear. It has no logical coherence, and it does not really propose a Biblical and confessional strategy to which we should adhere when we approach ecumenical organizations and other churches" (Feb. 2, 1987). One cannot help agreeing with these criticisms. The Synod felt that way too. It amended the Charter at several points in order to clarify and sharpen the language. The Charter as it came from the Interchurch Relations Committee featured the ingratiatingly vague, high-sounding language that has characterized many deliverances of those captivated by ecumenical expectations and hopes. The church surely has a legitimate ecumenical task, but this is not to be carried out in such a way that confessional integrity is put at risk.

Another phase of the ecumenical adventurism engaging the Interchurch Relations Committee is its continuing promotion of closer ties with the Reformed Church in America. The writer is not of a mind to say that the one church is all bad and the other is all good. By no means. The two churches have grown more similar in that neither communion seems to excel in clarity and unity of direction and purpose today. What could union between these two denominations be expected to accomplish? A stronger, more united Reformed church? That is seriously to be doubted. In fact, such prospect would have to be called a fantasy. To those who are assiduously promoting closer ties between the two churches a word of caution seems in order. If such union should come about, it is altogether likely that this ecumenical dream would not come to fruition in one united church, but would rather shatter into four pieces, namely, (1) a communion of the more progressive or liberal element in both churches; (2) a communion of the confessional or conservative element in both churches; (3) a communion of those who would keep the Reformed Church in America as it is; and (4) a communion of those who would keep the Christian Reformed Church as it is. Is this what the Interchurch Relations Committee wants? Or perhaps the dream would shatter into just two pieces, namely, numbers (1) and (2) above. If confusion and lack of clear Reformed direction should continue to prevail in

both denominations, then such a development might bring blessing to all concerned.

The High Seriousness of the Christian's Struggle

Still another sympton of the troubled state of the Christian
Reformed Church today is one less dramatic or obvious than
those already mentioned, but that is nevertheless a matter of
importance that could well insinuate itself more and more into
the life of the church. It has to do with the interpretation of
the seventh chapter of the book of Romans. In this passage
the apostle Paul speaks of the intense struggle between the
Christian's longing to serve God on the one hand and the rem-
nants of the sinful nature on the other.

There has long been a sharp debate among Christians regarding this chapter, especially verses 13-25. The central issue
in this debate has been the question whether Paul speaks in
this passage of his pre-conversion experience or of his post-
conversion, Christian life. In other words, is the intense struggle described in Romans seven part of regenerate life or
unregenerate life?

Reformed students of Scripture have generally followed the
teaching that the struggle described so grippingly in Romans
7 is normal for the Christian. The following familiar names appear among those who have held to this view: Augustine (in
later life), Calvin, Luther, C. Hodge, A. A. Hodge, Alford,
Bavinck, Kuyper, Berkhof, Berkouwer, Murray, Greijdanus, Len-
ski, Hendriksen and Bruce.[6] The Heidelberg Catechism plainly
teaches this view in Question-Answers 60, 62, 114 and 115.
(References to Romans 7 should be noted among the prooftexts).
Chapter XIII of the Westminster Confession also gives expression to this view. The celebrated allegory on the Christian life
by the Puritan author John Bunyan entitled *Pilgrim's Progress*
depicts the struggling Christian as he fights many temptations
and trials on his way to the Celestial City.

In more recent times some Reformed scholars have questioned this common interpretation of Romans 7. One of these

---

[6]For some of the names of this list of Bible interpreters I am
indebted to Wm. Hendriksen's commentary on the book of Romans,
pp. 229-30.

is the late Anthony A. Hoekema of Calvin Seminary, whose book *The Christian Looks At Himself* (1975) argued for the view that in Romans 7 Paul is speaking of his pre-conversion experience. Also breaking with the customary Reformed position on Romans 7 are Herman Ridderbos of The Netherlands and Hoekema's colleague at Calvin Seminary, Andrew Bandstra.[7] Finding that many Christians have a very negative self-image, one not reflecting the joy and peace of salvation from sin in Christ, Hoekema came to the conclusion that Romans 7 with Paul's lament "Wretched man that I am" needed a new look. It goes beyond the bounds of this writing to enter into a detailed study of the contents and argumentation of Dr. Hoekema's book. A thorough critique, written by Willis De Boer of Calvin College, appeared in the *Calvin Theological Journal* of November 1977.

In chapter six I referred to the fact that the editor of *The Banner* also took this position in 1985. Thus this deviation from the teaching of the Heidelberg Catechism and from the usual Reformed position has taken on some strength in the Christian Reformed Church. With two professors at Calvin Seminary espousing this deviant view, it is highly likely that the pulpit of the church has been affected. In fact, the present writer is aware of concrete evidence to that effect. By and large the Christian Reformed Church has nurtured a body of people who are sensitive to the requirements of God's moral law and responsive to God's call to holiness. Romans 7 has long been for believers a clear reminder of the intense struggle the Christian experiences as he, "still inclined to all evil." learns "more and more to know our sinful nature," and strives with prayer "to God for the grace of the Holy Spirit, to be renewed more and more after the image of God" (Heidelberg Catechism, 60, 115). Furthermore, he has heard from the pulpit may calls for "daily conversion," and has also heard series of sermons on Ephesians 6 about putting on "the whole armor of God" in order to carry on the struggle against the evil one and all his forces. Such preaching if truly faithfully done, could only reinforce the listener's perception that the intense struggle of Romans 7 should be seen as a description of his own Christian experience.

---

[7] See *The Banner*, Sept. 23, 1985, p. 5.

In dealing with the admonition of I Peter 1:16, "Be holy, because I am holy," while teaching a Bible class of some twenty mature Christians from several different denominational backgrounds, I asked the class how they felt about the notion that Romans 7 did not apply to the experience of the Christian. The first reaction was one of mild surprise that such teaching was seriously considered among Christians. Then, more to the point, was the response that to take Romans 7 out of the Christian's experience would mean a weakening of the Christian's sense of his spiritual struggle against temptations within and without. All the members of the class shared this opinion of the relevance of Romans 7 to their lives.

Does the prevailing Reformed understanding of Romans 7 necessarily lead to an overblown sense of guilt that makes for a sickly negativism and a bleak self-image? Not at all. Romans 7 also rings with Paul's jubilant cry, "Thanks be to God — through Jesus Christ our Lord!" And a good dosage of the grand teaching of justification by faith alone in pure grace, on the basis of Christ's complete and perfect work, should dispel all sickly, negativistic self-images. Perhaps a better, more sensitive preaching of the authentic Biblical message of the Catechism is called for, a message that accentuates the riches of salvation in Christ, riches that come to expression in grateful, obedient, Spirit-led, joyous living.

On the other hand, adopting the non-catechism notion of Romans 7 can only mean a lessening of the drive to sanctification. In fact, such teaching, should it gain ground in the church, can be expected to contribute to the rise of a deceptive, superficial triumphalism that is badly out of step with the hard facts of the Christian's struggle to serve his Lord and King in all areas of life to the glory of God. We are saved to serve God in obedience. Undercutting the will to obey is always the old nature still active in us. That old nature must be resisted at all costs, by the power of the Spirit working in us. That makes for spiritually disciplined Christians who rise above the blandness and the lethargy that can so quickly make us poor servants of Jesus Christ. We have a battle on our hands — always. That fact keeps us on our toes spiritually.

When Paul spoke as he did in Romans 7, about doing what he didn't want to do and not doing what he willed to do ("What a wretched man I am!"), he always carried in his soul the dark memory of his life as a rampaging persecutor of Jesus Christ. That dark chapter of his life was part of him, and it always formed the background of the awareness of his sinfulness. That is clear from his writing in I Timothy 1:15, where he said, "I am the worst of sinners." (Note well that he said "I am," not "I was." The Greek text plainly has "I am"). In the context of this heartfelt confession Paul speaks of himself as "once a blasphemer and a persecutor and a violent man." But the context is also rich in references to the amazing grace that "Our Lord poured out on me abundantly." The splendor of the grace of God shines most brilliantly when the sinner knows himself to be the "worst," a "wretched man." Awareness of this fact lifts the word *grace* out of the dictionary and out of the theological classroom into its role as a living fire in the soul of a child of God as he fights the good fight against the world, the flesh and the devil.

The Non-Payment of Quotas

A symptom of the deep unrest in the Christian Reformed Church is the non-payment of quotas by a sizable number of congregations. Such payments are the monies that a congregation, depending on its size, pays toward the maintenance of denominational programs, such as world missions, home missions, Back To God Hour, Calvin College and Seminary, and others. This program of quota support has long been a source of stability and strength in the church. These quotas, agreed to each year by synod, are not looked upon as a tax or assessment, but congregations are under a strong compulsion to make these payments faithfully. This program has reflected a oneness of faith and purpose that could only be seen as a symbol of a strong, united church. Today this fine program is in deep trouble. If reports coming to the writer are correct, a considerable number of churches have taken the drastic step of withholding some or all quota payments to the denomination-wide causes. It is to be doubted that any church council takes such a step readily or lightly. The payment of quotas has a deeply entrenched place in the life and practice of the Christian Reformed Church. There have been and are reasons other than protest why churches do not pay their quota share. But the non-payment of quotas in recent years has been prompted mainly because the church council (or at times an individual member) could no longer in good conscience support some program(s) of the denomination. Such non-payment has reflected profound dissatisfaction with the state of the church.

CHAPTER 9
From Confusion and Uncertainty To What?

Where is all the confusion and uncertainty leading the Christian Reformed Church? Listen to what a sympathetic outside observer has said about the state of affairs in the Christian Reformed Church. After commenting on the disintegration of authority that has taken place in the Roman Catholic Church since Vatican II, Nathan O. Hatch, Director of Graduate Studies in the Department of History at Notre Dame University, had this to say, "The Catholic experience is symptomatic of a much broader trend: that powerful and synthetic theologies are everywhere on the wane. A similar if less drastic, toppling of a given systematic theology is taking place within the Christian Reformed Church and among other Calvinists. A stable theological system which for generations had been the intellectual core of broader intellectual life has been losing its grip over the last twenty-five years — parts being laid aside, others simply ignored."[1] Is this assessment correct? It appears to be very much in line with what we have been exploring in these chapters. What lies ahead for the church?

This is a troubling question. It should be faced honestly. Such honesty requires a fair evaluation of the Christian Reformed Church. The writer is not of a mind to say that the situation is all bad with the church and therefore hopeless. Not at all. There is much that the members of the church can rejoice in. There is reason for joyful gratitude in the fact that there are many members who want their church to remain true to her character as a Reformed church bound together by a common faith as that is set forth in the three Forms of Unity. I suspect that a majority of the members share this desire. Then there is the fine ministry of the Back To God Hour as it proclaims

---

[1]*The Reformed Journal,* Sept. 1985, p. 14.

the Word faithfully worldwide in many different languages in the context of today's problems, hurts and concerns. The church has lost much of its isolation from the world's problems and needs. Its sense of ministry has grown greatly. It has a commendable program of World Missions,[2] and of world-wide relief. The denomination also has an aggressive program of domestic missions.

These positive elements in the total picture are indeed cause for rejoicing. But there are other elements in the total picture. There are not only the matters that have been discussed in the preceding chapters; there is also the instruction we receive from modern church history. There is no reason to doubt that the so-called mainline churches of North America could have been described at some point in their respective histories in much the same way that the Christian Reformed Church is depicted in the preceding paragraph. And very much to the point is the history of the Reformed Churches in the Netherlands (De Gereformeerde Kerken in Nederland), the church that mothered so many members of the Christian Reformed Church. What a great, solid church that once was. Yet look at it today. Any number of qualified observers have reported that in many respects it is in sorry shape. It continues to hold membership in the World Council of Churches. Decisions have been made on the place of homosexuals in the fellowship of the church that are based more on psychological and sociological considerations than on the teaching of the Bible. A classis granted approval for the baptism of the child adopted by a lesbian couple. That academic jewel of which the Reformed people of the Netherlands were once so justifiably proud, the Free University of Amsterdam, is today lost to the cause of the Reformed faith, the faith that gave birth to the school. And we mention once more that thoroughly relativistic document adopted by the church entitled *God With Us*.

---

[2]In 1970 I made a study of the ratio of foreign missionaries to the number of church members in four denominations, namely, what was then the Presbyterian Church in the U.S. (southern Presbyterian), Reformed Church in America, Southern Baptist Church, and the Christian Reformed Church. I found the last-named to have the highest ratio.

Will the Christian Reformed Church follow in the same dismal path, a path taken by so many churches and church-related institutions in modern times? Let no one hide his head in the cozy sands of blind institutional loyalty. There are ominous danger signals. What can be expected when in the picture we see a flawed conception of Biblical authority, faulty usages of the Bible in addressing issues in the church, outright departures from the teaching of the creeds, wanton disregard of the requirements of the solemnly avowed Form of Subscription, the teaching of evolution in the church's officially maintained college, ecumenical adventurism that puts the church's confessional stance at risk, loose handling of the Church Order, disregard for the sensitivities of many troubled members, and a drift toward a top-heavy bureaucracy in the government of the church?

Liberalism

Does the writer mean to say that the Christian Reformed Church is going liberal? Do the various matters mentioned in the preceding paragraph spell liberalism? Here we have to exercise some care. Words like *liberal* and *liberalism* are loaded words and many pages could be devoted to what these words mean. It should be pointed out, first of all, that not all deviations for the doctrinal standards of the church signify liberalism. Such deviation may mean that a person or group is drifting toward that confessionally ill-defined mentality called fundamentalism or evangelicalism. Such attitudes cannot be described as liberal. Nor can they be described as Reformed, although the newer term evangelicalism reflects thinking that is somewhat less unacceptable to those of Reformed persuasion than the older term fundamentalism.

In the series of articles that the Rev. Clarence Boomsma wrote in 1973-75 about the Christian Reformed Church (see chapter 3), he made reference to a movement in the church that he called *cautious liberalization*. About this movement he said, "Those in the church who possess a more progressive spirit, maintain that we cannot remain unchanged in a changing world if we are to survive in and speak meaningfully to the world. They believe we must face the issues which are raised for the Christian faith and its Reformed interpretation by modern learning and science, and be prepared to rethink our fallible understanding of the infallible truth."[3] Boomsma indicated in his series that he did not want to use the word liberal in speaking of those in the church who promoted this cautious liberalization. He preferred the word progressive. His reason for this choice was that he wanted to avoid being understood as using the word liberal in the sense that J. Gresham Machen used it in his widely read book *Christianty and Liberalism.* In this book Machen used the term liberalism in its full-blown sense of naturalism over against the supernaturalism of Christianity. G. C. Berkouwer of Amsterdam used the word in much the same way in his book *Modern Uncertainty and Christian Faith.* In the chapter entitled "Old and New Protestantism" the Dutch theologian describes the New Protestantism with the words *modernism* and *liberalism.* As an illustration of this New Protestantism he told the story of a professor at the University of Leiden who declared in class that in the light of modern science it was impossible to speak of the resurrection of Jesus Christ from the dead. All the students in the class expressed their agreement with the professor's bold assertion by applauding. One of those who applauded was Abraham Kuyper. This noted theologian and leader, later converted from his university-bred liberalism, lived to regret the dishonor he had done to his Lord.[4]

Boomsma was correct in not using the word liberal as just defined in speaking of those who sought "cautious liberalization" of the church. Is it, then, wholly inappropriate and unfair to use the word liberal in speaking of the erosion of confessional commitment in the Christian Reformed Church? Not necessarily. James D. Bratt's fascinating study *Dutch Calvinism In Modern America* gives us some help as to the proper use of the word liberal in our evaluation of trends in the Christian Reformed Church. Bratt sees in the recent history of the church a contest between two camps that he labels Confessionalists (or Conservatives) and Progressives. With this division in the church in mind he discusses in some detail the controversy

---

[3]*The Banner,* Sept. 14, 1973, p. 14.
[4]*Modern Uncertainty and Christian Faith,* 1953, pp. 29-30.

over the views of Professor Dekker of Calvin Seminary (a controversy referred to earlier in chapter three). This case occupied the attention of the church for some years prior to its conclusion in 1967, when the Synod, in extended session, produced a feeble decision that settled virtually nothing. About this dispute and its mousy settlement Bratt declared, "The Confessionalists' dominance was now broken on the official level."[5] This evaluation is much the same as that which appeared elsewhere in 1981, when it was observed that the conservatives in the church were not in the driver's seat, and could best be "compared to back seat drivers."[6]

What is especially significant in the historian's reflection on this doctrinal dispute is the following commentary: "Nor was the scent of protoliberalism entirely imaginary in the Dekker case. The progressives' insistence that 'faith' be separated from 'theology,' that the intelligentsia be allowed more latitude for discussion, that cases be settled slowly and in good order, that traditional terminology cover new meanings, that the creeds be regarded in their historical conditioning as testimonies to as well as statements of the truth, all had ample precedent in the early stages of liberalism some ninety years before" (*Ibid*, p. 208). Whatever one may think of the individual items in this citation, it is clear that, in Bratt's judgment, the extended debate over this doctrinal issue bore evidence of learnings toward liberalism. Also noteworthy is Bratt's judgment that R. B. Kuiper, in his writings on Professor Dekker's views, "saw the progressives imposing on Scripture a logic . . . that stemmed from incipient liberalism" (*Ibid*, p. 207).[7]

---

[5]*Dutch Calvinism In Modern America*, 1984, p. 207. Bratt fails to mention the fact that the issue came back to synod in 1968 by way of appeals from three consistories, appeals which asked for clarification of the language used in the 1967 decision. Synod 1968 issued a statement that to some extent met the concern of the appellants. (*Acts of Synod 1968*, pp. 75-76).

[6]*The Outlook*, Nov. 1981, pp. 2-3.

[7]The words "liberalism" or "incipient liberalism" do not appear in the writings of R. B. Kuiper referred to by Bratt. However, he may well have such words as these in view: "to identify the divine love for all men with God's love for his elect is to invite the gravest sort of heterodoxy" (*The Outlook*, March 1963, p. 8).

So we have the three words or phrases, namely, "cautious liberalization," "protoliberalism," and "incipient liberalism." It should be observed that these three expressions have been taken from the writings of people who are, to all appearances, sympathetic with the position of those called "progressives," or who are at least not hostile to the position. It would have been easy to pick out instances of the use of words like liberal and liberalism from writings of people not sympathetic with the point of view of the progressives. But such citations would not, for obvious reasons, be particularly persuasive in the context of the present discussion.

What shall we make of these three expressions? They mean, to put it candidly and simply, that we have the beginnings of liberalism in the Christian Reformed Church. That statement is inaccurate. In Dr. Bratt's opinion the beginnings of liberalism were present almost a quarter century ago. And modern church history teaches us that, if God does not in his mercy intervene, liberalism in the sense in which Machen and Berkouwer spoke of it will in time have indisputable sway in the Christian Reformed Church. Let no one be shocked by that statement. Let no naive and sentimental loyalty blind our eyes. The development of "cautious liberalization" and "protoliberalism" into full-blown liberalism has happened time and again. It is happening in the Gereformeerde Kerken in Nederland today. Many readers of this book know well a non-Reformed church in downtown Grand Rapids whose pulpit once rang with the good news of the gospel of God's saving grace in Jesus Christ. Then liberalism began to creep in, and the time came when the message from that pulpit became outright naturalism, with the supernaturalism of Christianity wholly abandoned. Let no Christian Reformed loyalist say, "It can't happen here."

We do well to take note of the reason that Boomsma gave for the "cautious liberalization" that he talked about. As we observed earlier in this chapter, he said of the Progressives in the church, "They believe we must face the issues which are raised for the Christian faith and its Reformed interpretation by modern learning and science." That is the reason usually given for the rise of liberalism. Said Berkouwer in his 1952 Calvin Foundation Lectures, "All modernists and liberals view the orthodoxy of the Reformation as an untenable position which is no longer on the level of our times and which does not recognize the achievements of modern science and the modern world-view."[8]

Liberalism does not enter a church in its full-blown form. And it does not enter with the blare of trumpets. It enters unobtrusively, gradually, often with the appearance of truth, or at least plausibility. It enters by way of seemingly small deviations from the church's creedal teaching, by way of disregard of the Form of Subscription, by way of preaching more about human needs and aspiriations than about God's grace and glory, by way of questionable notions of academic freedom, by way of failure to see that the truth of God's Word transcends cultural changes. It comes in also by way of very well written materials whose literary excellence may interfere with the reader's seeing the potential for harm in such materials. Here I refer again to the important series of articles on the "Mind of the Church" written in connection with the centennial of the Christian Reformed Church (see Chapter 3). These articles took a dim view of the "mind of safety," which is exercised about preserving the church's legacy of truth. The "militant mind," the mind that would fight to protect the church's legacy, was criticized sharply and at length. The articles espoused the "positive mind," the mind whose "all-controlling word" is love. Though the author hedged his argument with many impressive qualifiers and with a number of most acceptable statements of truth, I have to say with some reluctance that, in my judgment, the articles constituted a fitting recipe for liberalism.

The New Hermeneutic and the Heidelberg Catechism

Liberalism is also promoted by writings and speeches which undercut the role of the creeds in the life of the church. The Christian Reformed Church has a stipulation in the Church Order that says, "At one of the services each Lord's Day, the minister shall ordinarily preach the Word as summarized in the Heidelberg Catechism, following its sequence" (Article 54b). By this means one of the creeds of the church is kept before the people and is not virtually forgotten as it is tucked away in the back of the church's praisebook.

---

[8]*Modern Uncertainty and Christian Faith*, pp. 25f.

In *The Banner* of February 27, 1989, an article appeared challenging this rule of the church. "Why have this article?" the author of the piece asked. "The church needs to think about revising the catechism-preaching rule in a way that takes into account the changes that have occurred since the sixteenth century."

The author's main line of argument is interesting. This begins with a quotation from Cornelius Plantinga's *A Place To Stand.* In speaking of the call of Elector Frederick III of the Palatinate in Germany for the writing of a catechism, Plantinga is quoted as saying, "He thought he might do this by settling on sound, biblical answers to the hardest questions being disputed" among Lutherans, Zwinglians, Anabaptists and Reformed believers. The author of the *Banner* article says that Frederick III "desperately sought to resolve this unhappy situation" among disputing groups of Christians.

Does not this approach call for some correction? This approach seems to suggest that in calling for a catechism Frederick's purpose was mainly polemical, that is, to furnish correct answers to the "hardest questions" in dispute. Is this emphasis correct? From the reading that I have done the impression is gained that Frederick, who, after much study of the Bible and a good deal of soul-searching, had come to embrace the Reformed position as the biblical one. Consequently he wanted a catechism as a tool for teaching the true faith to the young and also as a guide for preaching. In the writing of the Catechism Ursinus and Olevianus dealt with certain hard questions, especially about the Lord's Supper, and the extended treatment of this subject in the Catechsim gives evidence of their wrestling with these "hard questions." But other than that the Catechism gives far more evidence of concern for a positive delineation of the teaching of the Bible than it does for settling disputes among contending parties.

Having introduced the subject in this debatable manner, the author of the article in *The Banner* goes on to argue that the Catechism, having been written to deal with the matters that were pressing in the sixteenth century, is hardly suitable for dealing with the issues of our times. "Historical events have drastically changed our traditional landscape," we are told. Reference is made to the Holocaust, the Second Vatican Council, Jewish-Christian dialogue, and reforms in the Roman Catholic

Church. Then this is added, "In addition, we now face problems the authors of the catechism could not have dreamed about — problems like world hunger, the threat of nuclear war, pollution, overpopulation, and technological change. The original intent of the catechism was to address the hardest questions in the sixteenth century, especially questions relating to the Lord's Supper. Today's hardest questions are not the same as those of four centuries ago."

This line of argument is open to serious question. It has to be challenged, and that on two counts. In the first place, as has already been stressed, the catechism was intended to be a positive statement of the teaching of the Bible. It was not intended to present solutions to the "hardest questions" of the times except insofar as such questions had to do with biblical teaching.

In the second place, the historical-cultural developments that the article mentions are not the kinds of problems that the Catechism set out to deal with. There is no evidence of any intent that the Catechism would deal with the questions relating to world developments. These things were simply outside of the Catechism's purview. And, note this, there were dramatic world developments at that time and place. The world was exploding before the eyes of the writers of the Heidelberg Catechism. A whole new world had been discovered. Magellan and Francis Drake were names to be reckoned with as intrepid travelers who made fantastic journeys in this vastly expanded world. Forty years before the Catechism was published Magellan had led sailing vessels on a three-year journey around the world. Here was proof positive that the world was round.

There were more such dramatic developments in those days. There was an explosion of information and knowledge due to the invention in Europe of printing with movable type. In the academic world nature was moving to the fore as the proper object of study for man, to take the place of the theological and metaphysical concerns which had occupied the scholasticism that had dominated the academic world for centuries. And finally, to mention just one more such dramatic development, twenty years before the Catechism appeared on the scene in 1563 Nicolaus Copernicus of Poland published his book *Concerning the Revolutions of the Celestial Spheres*. This event sparked the so-called "Copernican Revolution," which reversed the traditional thinking that the earth's position was fixed and that the heavenly bodies rotated around it.

All of these dramatic developments were going on at the time the Catechism was written, developments which were, relatively speaking, on a par with the modern problems that the author of the article mentions as rendering the Catechism largely irrelevant today. Yet there is, to the best of my knowledge, no indication of these profoundly significant historical developments in the Catechism. The Catechism sets forth the central teaching of the Bible, a teaching that transcends the changes that come and go on the restless sea of history.

The *Banner* article under discussion failed to demonstrate, in its main line of argumentation, that catechismal preaching has become irrelevant in the Christian Reformed Church. The article was an effort to apply the "new hermeneutic" to the Heidelberg Catechism." The expression *new hermeneutic* has not been used previously in this book, although this interpretative device was used in some of the discussions dealt with, especially the matter of women in office. The new hermeneutic concentrates on the role of culture and history in the interpretation of the text of an historical document. It can be applied to any piece of literature, although its application to the Bible is a matter of special concern to the church. The interpretation of the Bible is of greater and more serious interest because in the text of Scripture we are dealing with writing that the church confesses to be the very Word of God.

In the use of the new hermeneutic men ask questions like these: what did the text mean when it was written? What was the cultural-historical situation when it was written? How did such cultural-historical factors affect the meaning of the text? What is the meaning of the text today? Is the text as written still meaningful today? If so, in what sense? Did the historical-cultural situation that prevailed when the text was written limit the text to that setting so that it is no longer relevant at a later time in a different historical-cultural setting? The application of this interpretative device to the Heidelberg Catechism did not come off, we have seen. It did not mainly because the Catechism, the church believes, faithfully reflects the teaching of God's infallible Word.

* * * * *

The beginnings of liberalism, we have ascertained, have been at work in the Christian Reformed Church for a quarter century. Does that mean the church has by now moved farther down that treacherous path, a path followed by so many churches in the past and also in our time? Is it still possible to heed a warning given to the church some thirty years ago by a very clear-minded churchman? Speaking of departures from the faith and using the Latin that he knew so well, he said, "And so I plead with you: *Principiis obstemus*. Let us withstand beginnings! *Principiis diligentur obstemus!* Let us diligently withstand beginnings! *Principiis diligentissime obstemus!* Let us most diligently withstand beginnings!"[9]

The article from which this eloquent warning was taken was speaking about heresy, and the alert was aimed at the beginnings of heresy in the church. Has this earnest alert become passe? In the issue of February 2, 1987, *The Banner's* answer-man declared, "Epithets such as *heretic* fortunately are not an integral part of our vocabulary today?" Was this opinion correct? The whole answer to the questioner's inquiry made clear that the word heretic has to be used with care. We would hesitate to use the word, for example, of one who rejected the practice of infant baptism even as he wholeheartedly subscribed to the truth of the Bible and embraced Jesus Christ as his Savior and Lord. But such proper care in the use of the word heretic is something less than saying that the word is no longer an "integral part" of the church's vocabulary. If that is the case, then the grim truth is that liberalism has taken over in the church. The author of this startling statement exercised a leadership role for many years in the affairs of the Publications Board of the Christian Reformed Church.

Did not the Christian Reformed Church produce a statement recently that could be said to give current and proper expression to the church's faith? I refer to the *Contemporary Testimony* named "Our World Belongs To God," adopted by the Synod of 1986 and appearing in the back pages of the new Psalter Hymnal (c1987). Just what this document will mean

---

[9]R. B. Kuiper in Heerema, *RB A Prophet In The Land*, 1986, p. 190.

121

in the continuing history of the denomination remains to be seen. To this date it is not apparent that the Testimony's place in the church is a significant one. Though well written with many impressive and even eloquent lines in it, the document suffers from a lack of precision in thought and adequacy of formulation that could be expected to mark a writing of this kind, done in free verse.

A very basic question is already suggested by the title. What does the word *world* mean? The reference to Psalm 24:1 is hardly enough to validate the use of the expression "our world" when so frequently in the New Testament the *world* is represented as being in hostility to God.[10] And just where do we find express warrant for the notion that it is the mission of the church "to tell the news that our world belongs to God"? The construction of paragraph 44 with its punctuation (dashes) and the reference to Matthew 28:18-20 suggest this interpretation of the Testimony at this point.

Furthermore, paragraph 44 seems to say that "to feed the hungry" is part of the gospel that the church, following the apostles, "is sent" to spread abroad. One has to like the emphasis on the need to feed the hungry. That is surely an important part of the task of Christians in the world. But is feeding the hungry part of the good news (gospel) that the church is called to proclaim? And if feeding the hungry is seen as being of the very character of "disciples" who must be taught to "obey everything" Christ has commanded (Matt. 28:20), then why is just this one facet of such discipleship selected out of the full range of spiritual-ethical responsibilities Christ has laid upon

---

[10]A question about the Testimony keeps pressing itself upon me, namely, has this composition been influenced by what is called by some "realized eschatology"? This type of thinking holds that the Kingdom of our Lord has already come in its fullness, whereas the view among Reformed students generally is that, yes, the Kingdom has in a very real sense already come but its fullness will not come until our Lord returns. That fullness belongs to the "not yet" of the Kingdom. The words of Revelation 11:15 should be seen as being part of that "not yet." These words are, "The kingdom of the world has become the kingdom of our Lord and of his Christ, and he will reign forever and ever." (See A. A. Hoekema, *The Bible and the Future*, Eerdmans, c1979, pp. 293-297).

his followers? Why not stress Christ's teaching regarding the two great commandments on which "depend all the law and the prophets"?

Paragraph 55 on peace-keeping seems lacking in clarity. Are we "following the Prince of Peace" (James 3:18 is the reference text) when we "call on our governments to work for peace" and that we declare that "we deplore the arms race"? Is not more careful definition called for here? Of what peace is Jesus the Prince? Of course, we all deplore the arms race. But what of any real significance are we saying to our government when our elected officials have to make hard decisions regarding weapons "needed in the defense of justice and freedom," and for the protection of the citizens in a dangerous world?

Questions such as these surface as we peruse this Testimony, thus reducing its usefulness as a meaningful statement of what the church stands for and as a fitting instrument for conveying such to the world around us. In the final analysis the Testimony too leaves us with a considerable measure of confusion and uncertainty.

Postscript

This letter got rather long, Mother. There were so many things I wanted to talk about with you. Perhaps there are things of importance that others might think should have been brought up. If I have omitted something really important, I hope I shall be forgiven.

Now that we have spoken of these many things, what is the upshot of it all? We have spoken much of confusion and uncertainty in the family. Under such conditions it was not surprising that we detect a drift away from what the family has always thought it stood for. That commentary about our family by a friendly observer has troubled me a lot. He said in part, as quoted in chapter nine, "A stable theological system which for generations has been the intellectual core of broader intellectual life has been losing its grip over the past twenty-five years." That comment deserves much careful reflection. It means, as I see it, that at its center our family is no longer governed by a strong God-centered Calvinism.

That is why I have written, Mother. A precious legacy is fading. So I am asking you to do a lot of thinking about just who you are. Don't you know any more who you are? Have you lost your sense of identity? Are you suffering from an ecclesiastical type of Alzheimer's Disease? Families and individuals find their identity first of all in their roots. No person or family or institution that cuts its ties with its roots can hope to be spiritually healthy and strong. We cannot expect to meet the challenges of today and tomorrow unless we have a clear idea as to who we are and what we stand for. One of the great anthropologists of this century, Margaret Mead, once said in my hearing that there is nothing so certain in this modern age as the certainty of change. Have you been thrown off balance by these winds of change, Mother? The members of our family would do well to utter the words of a familiar hymn as a prayer —

> Change and decay in all around I see;
> O Thou who changest not, abide with me.

Not only would I urge you to think seriously about your identity, but also in the second place, I would urge the members of the family to give serious thought to a closely related matter, namely, our theological health. Please look again at the commentary on our theological situation quoted in the second paragraph of this postscript. In theology we deal with this fundamental question: Who is God and how are we in the totality of our lives related to him? Since 1924 the church has let stand without correction or expansion an admittedly inadequate statement of an important element of Christian doctrine, that which goes by the name of Common Grace. By its failure to refine and expand the three simple points adopted in 1924, even when such refinement was expressly called for, the church tacitly accepted a lowered standard of doing theology. Then, in 1952 the upheaval at the seminary profoundly affected our theological health when the makeup of the theological leadership in the family was changed.

These two developments, discussed in chapters 2 and 3 of this letter, form a background for evaluating the theological health of the church in the last decades. It should be apparent that for the most part what has happened theologically in the family has turned around one central point, namely, the understanding of the nature and the application of the authority of the Bible. In this letter I have tried to show how faulty understanding and use of the Bible appeared in the study report on Biblical Authority (chapter 4), in the study report on Office and Ordination (chapter 5), in the handling of the women in office issue, in the failure of the church to deal more firmly with the teaching of evolution in Calvin College, and in the church's handling of an overture that sought clarification on the question of the cultural conditioning of the Bible (chapter 6). Also, Articles II-VII of the Confession of Faith were not truly honored in these matters. We have always been a people of the Word. If many troubling questions surround that Word as to its authority and application, then the Word is no longer our sure guide and we are in great danger of losing our identity and character. And we are in great danger of losing our witness to an age of intellectual and moral relativism.

In the third place all members of the family should deal respectfully and graciously with one another. The family is not hierarchical. We have neither pope nor college of cardinals. The family is deeply committed to the principle of the universal priesthood of all believers. Sometimes humble, thoroughly dedicated members of the family are more to be trusted than those in positions of leadership. There may be no arrogance of any kind, be it academic or bureaucratic. Nor should there be a self-willed promotion of an agenda for change without due regard for the feelings of all. There must be great care, self-restraint and love exercised by all, in humble obedience to our Lord and his Word, lest our family break apart, to the hurt of all.

May God bless you, Mother. Our family cannot remain indefinitely in a state taut polarization. The ties that bind us together will break unless we work hard at those things that must be done, things such as those suggested above. This does not mean that we refrain from speaking plainly. We must speak plainly, and in love. This I have sought to do. May God look with favor on this effort of mine. I have written as I have, Mother, because I love you.

APPENDIX A
The Florida Overture

Classis Florida overtures the Synod of 1985 to request of the Rev. Andrew Kuyvenhoven, editor of *The Banner*, according to the terms of the Form of Subscription, a further explanation of his understanding of the Confession of Faith, Articles V and VII, in view of the following writing by our brother in *The Banner* of January 23, 1984:

> There is no doubt in my mind that Paul was prescribing a restricted role to women in the service of worship when he wrote I Corinthians 14:34 and I Timothy 2:12.
>
> However, the reason for the restrictions were local, cultural, and therefore temporal. Paul could appeal to what was in his day a common moral judgment: a woman speaking in church looked "bad," "shameful" (I Cor. 14:35). But when such an appeal can no longer be made, the special apostolic prescription is also removed.
>
> In other words, the veil, the head covering, long hair, and other prescriptions had a cultural importance they no longer have. But reverence, submission, and the good name of the Christian community are the enduring concerns of these passages.

Note: The same thinking about the Bible and culture was expressed in an editorial in *The Banner* of May 14, 1984, and in a speech on "Bible and Culture" given by Rev. Kuyvenhoven on October 12, 1984 as reported in the *Outlook* of January 1985.

Grounds:
1. The exegesis whereby Rev. Kuyvenhoven sets aside the plain overt teaching of the texts involved and limits the teaching of these passages to "reverence, submission and the good name of the Christian community" is plainly not valid.

   a. According to Rev. Kuyvenhoven the "reasons for the restrictions" were in the first place "local." We note that Paul says in I Corinthians 14:33-34, "*As in all the congregations of the saints,* women should remain silent in the churches" (italics added). The italicized words plainly assert that Paul is laying down a rule for all the churches and not for just one or two of them. It is highly unlikely that one could so familiarize himself with the "local" circumstances in "all the congregations of the saints" that he could declare that one of the reasons for Paul's restrictions is "local." But even more to the point is that the "reason" for Paul's restriction is found in God's Word and not in local circumstances, as the immediate context in both instances clearly shows.

    b. With the word "local" ruled out, the only remaining reasons for the Pauline restriction in I Corinthians 14:34 and I Timothy 2:12 are "cultural, and therefore temporal." Under the inspiration of the Holy Spirit, Paul finds the reason for his teaching in I Corinthians 14:34 in "the Law," which means the Old Testament or some part of it. And the reason for the teaching in I Timothy 2:12 is found in some of the earliest teaching of Scripture, namely, that "Adam was formed first, then Eve" (I Tim. 2:13). How can such teaching, deeply rooted in the abiding Word of God itself, be spoken of as "cultural, and therefore temporal?"

2. Article V of the Confession states that the books of the Bible are "for the regulation, foundation, and confirmation of our faith; believing without any doubt all things contained in them . . ." There can be no doubt that when the Confession was written and when it was adopted by the Reformed churches, the words of Article V covered I Corinthians 14:34 and I Timothy 2:12 in the plain and overt teaching of these passages. Rev. Kuyvenhoven has chosen to disagree with this testimony of the churches by dismissing as irrelevant today the express teaching of the two passages in question, for reasons that are exegetically invalid. Rev. Kuyvenhoven should therefore give further explanation of his understanding of Article V as it relates to I Corinthians 14:34 and I Timothy 2:12. To be sure, the plain and overt teaching of these passages must still be specifically interpreted, but that

is something other than dismissing such teaching as irrelevant.

3. Article VI of the Confession states that the "doctrine" (that is, teaching) of the Word of God "is most perfect and complete in all respects." How can the teaching of I Corinthians 14:34 and I Timothy 2:12 "be most perfect and complete in all respects" for us when the plain and overt teaching of these passages is declared to be irrelevant for us?

4. Article VII further states that we may not consider "custom . . . or succession of times and persons . . . of equal value with the truth of God." Rev. Kuyvenhoven should be called on to explain how that which he has written does not violate this language of Article VII, for he has said that the teaching of I Corinthians 14:34 and I Timothy 2:12 is a matter of customs and culture of the times in which Paul wrote. Since then the plain and overt teaching of these passages is said to reflect temporal cultural conditions ("succession of times and persons"), it follows that new customs and cultural conditions can set aside teaching of God's Word that is looked upon as bound up with earlier custom and culture. That makes "custom . . . or succession of times and persons . . . of equal value with the truth of God."

5. The need to ask Rev. Kuyvenhoven for further explanation of his views of certain articles of the Confession of Faith is reinforced by the fact that he has written about other articles of the Confession as follows: "The views of the Reformers are no longer ours. And the kind of thinking about the church that is recorded in the Belgic Confession is no longer functional in the Christian Reformed Church" (Editorial, *The Banner*, Oct. 26, 1981). The editor of our leading church paper has solemnly signified his persuasion "that all the articles and points of doctrine contained in the Confession . . . do fully agree with the Word of God" (Form of Subscription).

6. The issues raised in this overture are of great significance and should be faced by the church. These issues are disturbing to many in the church and are raising troublesome questions for them with respect to the Holy

Scriptures. What is to be understood by the cultural or temporal conditioning of the Bible? What does this mean in specific instances, like those raised by Rev. Kuyvenhoven? Does the acknowledgement of cultural and temporal conditioning mean that the Bible is a "time-bound" book, as Kuitert and others have alleged? How does Kuyvenhoven's teaching differ from the older liberalism, which said flatly that the Bible is out of date? These and similar questions must be dealt with for the sake of the peace and witness of our beloved church.

CLASSIS FLORIDA

Ralph A. Pontier
Stated Clerk

Done in meeting of Classis Florida January 23, 1985.

APPENDIX B
The Church's Witness and The Issue of Women In Office

The church's first responsibility in dealing with the issue of women in office was and is to ascertain the teaching of the Bible in the matter. A second area of responsibility deserves some comment. In a time when there is emphasis on the close tie that exists between the religious community and the culture in which it lives, the church should have directed, and should still direct, its attention also to the question of the kind of witness it brings to bear on the culture in which and to which it bears witness. Indeed, the testimony of one relatively small denomination would not in all likelihood have much impact on a troubled culture. But that is not the question. The question is rather this: does the church simply focus on its own internal affairs, or does it always also remember the world to which and in which it is called to witness?

In a world in which many women speak more of self-fulfillment than of self-giving, where there are women who seem to think it is their calling to do whatever men do, where women are being driven to the edge by trying to manage a tricky juggling act that seeks to balance the needs of the family with the demands of a job outside the home, where there are voices calling for a kindlier and gentler world—in such a world let the church of Jesus Christ point in the direction where blessing lies. Though the church may be only a voice crying in the wilderness of an increasingly ungodly and self-destructing society, let the "pillar and ground of the truth" concentrate its attention and that of those who will hear on those matters that are of highest importance.

Much more has to be said about the society in which and to which the church bears witness. It is a society given more and more to self-will, to demanding more and more for self, to regarding people and structures mainly as sources of gratification of personal wishes and fancies. It is a society that gives evidence of much lovelessness – as young people are caught up in an epidemic of suicide, as there are more and more broken homes, as teenage pregnancy has become a national scandal, as spouse-abuse and child-abuse have reached shocking levels, as hosts of people seek to fill their empty lives with drugs and alcohol, as a new and dreadful disease brought on largely by perverse and wanton sex grips the people with fear. It is a society that is groaning under the ever-increasing load of caring for those countless fellow citizens whose beginnings in life were pathetically flawed, or whose homes were broken, and so society gains hosts of members who never knew real love, never learned the meaning of responsibility, and never gained a true sense of self-respect.

In this society what should the church concentrate on in its witness? Of first importance, of course, is the message of the gospel of God's saving grace (love) in Christ. Next to that highest priority nothing is of greater importance than the unique and special task of *mothering,* mothering in the setting of a strong and loving family. I wish my church, in considering the role of women, had kept the broader picture in view instead of concentrating so narrowly on the parochial dimensions of the issue. Let the church make no determination which would in any way lessen our high and jealous regard for woman's special and unique place. There are all sorts of avenues of effective service that women can enter upon without becoming involved in those responsibilities which God has laid upon those to whom he has committed the duties of headship in the home and in the church.

The ravages of feminism in our time have been great. The original woman, listening to the arch-betrayer, wanted everything, and turmoil followed. Many of the modern daughters of Eve have learned from her, and one of their leaders said recently that their efforts would bring chaos. Let womanhood rediscover the two main functions which were originally committed to her, namely, that of being helpmeet to her mate, and that of being "mother of all the living." This original dual assignment was reinforced in the book of Proverbs, Chapter 31, where we read about the ideal woman who freely carries out her role as wife and mother in the home and outside it, to the joy and blessing of all. And our Lord himself also reinforced this teaching in all he said and did, as did the apostles after him.

Insensitive and cold is the person who cannot in some degree empathize with the woman who believes she is called to fill one of the special offices in the church. May she find a satisfying outlet for her talents and longings. At the same time the most important role for women is of such tremendous urgency for home, church and society that my empathy with the woman who seeks office has to be overruled in the greater and, I think, biblical perspective. This perspective is not made irrelevant in the case of the woman whose children have become adults and so she has come to a point in her life where she can attend to tasks outside the home without neglecting her primary responsibilities. The church's general rule, arrived at in obedience to Scripture and with an eye to the church's witness to the world, cannot accommodate the specifics of individual cases, especially when the general rule is of such importance and urgency. At the same time the sister, freed in large measure from her duties at home, can find satisfying avenues of service that bring glory to God and blessing to people as well as to herself. The reader should bear in mind that we are here speaking only of the performance of *official* functions in the church. What tasks a woman wishes to perform elsewhere is a question not dealt with in this discussion.